BUILD FROM NOW
HOW TO KNOW YOUR POWER, SEE YOUR ABUNDANCE & NOURISH THE WORLD

Damon Brown
www.DamonBrown.net
JoinDamon.me

TWITTER/INSTAGRAM: *@BROWNDAMON*
COACHING & SPEAKING REQUESTS:
DAMON@DAMONBROWN.NET

PUBLISHED BY:
Bring Your Worth

Build From Now
1st Edition
Copyright 2021 by Damon Brown
Edited by Jeanette Hurt
Cover designed by The Bec Effect
Cover photo by Alex Goetz

All rights reserved. Without limiting the rights under copyright reserved above, no part of this publication may be reproduced, stored in or introduced into a retrieval system, or transmitted, in any form, or by any means (electronic, mechanical, photocopying, recording, or otherwise) without the prior written permission of both the copyright owner and the above publisher of the book.

The author acknowledges the trademarked status and trademark owners of various products referenced in this work, which have been used without permission. The publication/use of these trademarks is not authorized, associated with, or sponsored by the trademark owners.

*To our young ancestor and our elder ancestor.
Thank you for leading the way.*

That which we do not bring to consciousness appears in our lives as fate.

Carl Jung

Table of Contents

Selected Books By The Author

I: An Outside Job

- The Low End of the Soup Bowl — 1
- Salmon — 15
- Your System is the Lock & Key — 43
- Understanding the FATEs — 63

II: An Inside Job

- How to Partner with Focus — 81
- How to Partner with Agility — 119
- How to Partner with Time — 155
- How to Partner with Energy — 189

III: Future's Past

- Here, You Forgot Something — 241

Take the Build From Now Quiz — 255

CONNECT WITH DAMON	**259**
AVAILABLE KEYNOTE TALKS	**263**
SIGNIFICANT REFERENCES	**267**
ACKNOWLEDGEMENTS	**287**
ABOUT THE AUTHOR	**291**

SELECTED BOOKS BY THE AUTHOR

BUILD FROM NOW:

LEVEL UP YOUR CREATIVE POWER, VALUE & SERVICE TO THE WORLD

THE ULTIMATE BITE-SIZED ENTREPRENEUR:

76 WAYS TO BOOST TIME, PRODUCTIVITY & FOCUS ON YOUR BIG IDEA

THE PASSIVE WRITER:

5 STEPS TO EARNING MONEY IN YOUR SLEEP

(W/ JEANETTE HURT)

OUR VIRTUAL SHADOW:

WHY WE ARE OBSESSED WITH DOCUMENTING OUR LIVES ONLINE

I
AN OUTSIDE JOB

The Low End of the Soup Bowl

The function, the very serious function of racism is distraction. It keeps you from doing your work. It keeps you explaining, over and over again, your reason for being.

Toni Morrison

Your 24 hours a day are not the same as mine.

There are headwinds that push against us. They are invisible, pervasive, and constant. Like air. They wrap around us and try to hold us tight. They want our resources. They want our strength. They want to keep us where we are.

The headwinds are as man-made as Hurricane Katrina. The storm was happenstance. The slipshod levee system is what created the damage. The barriers were made for cheap to better line government pockets. They were considered less consequential because the breach threatened poor, minority communities the most. Leadership already knew about the levee danger when I lived in my New Orleans apartment, as I biked thorough the nearby, beautiful 9th ward, eating, drinking, and bonding with the local artist community who had been there since Napoleon's troops stomped through.

This systemic neglect was a conscious choice. Certain people and their culturally-rich resources held less value than other neighborhoods and their populations. Therefore, they were starved of additional resources, such as peace of mind. It remains expensive to be poor. As I lived there in the year leading up to Katrina, literally everyone I met damn well knew we were in danger. "We are in a soup bowl," they'd tell me again and again. The French Quarter loomed as a raised lump in the middle. The upper-crust Garden District stood protected, too. The rest was fucked. How much extra effort does it take to do to, well, *anything*, if you know you're already fucked?

Nature designed New Orleans. Systemic choices designed the headwinds.

Not all headwinds are some natural phenomenon. Women are not born inferior leaders; in fact, New Zealand, Germany, and the handful of women-lead countries showed amazing guidance and smart containment during the 2020 coronavirus pandemic. Minorities are not naturally less-educated; recent studies show diverse C-suite leadership means better profits for businesses. And LGBTQ people are not culturally unsound; non-heteronormative-led family households create an environment as stable as, and often even more stable than heteronormative-led homes (Remember the oft-cited high American divorce rate was established well before gay marriage became legal. That's on straight people.).

These headwinds are formed by prejudice, guided with malice, and protected and maintained by systems. In Silicon Valley, they called it "pattern matching." Walk into a venture capitalist investor office looking like a young, straight white male, both cocky and antisocial, wearing a well-worn hoodie and ripped jeans, and freshly dropped out of an Ivy League school. As such, you look like you're cut from the same cloth as Mark Zuckerberg, Elon Musk, and the late patron saint of Silicon Valley, Steve Jobs. You don't need to keep explaining your reason for being. You don't need to allocate your precious resources to proving why you *belong* in the room. You can just be the best at what you do – and walk into the room. That's enough.

I founded my first startup in 2014 in San Diego, shortly after living as a tech journalist and author in Silicon Valley. It's not an exaggeration to say I was one degree away from all the active black founders in San Francisco. This culture was small and rich. We'd meet informally every Wednesday at our favorite watering hole. My friends, colleagues, and I would meet to share stories, support each other, and seed potential collaborations for the future.

In a CNN interview at the time, Silicon Valley tastemaker and TechCrunch founder Michael Arrington said, "I don't know any black founders." When pressed further, he said, "There's a guy, actually, his last company just launched at our event [TechCrunch Disrupt], and he's African American... But he could've launched a clown show onstage, and I would've put him up there, absolutely."

Ironically, as journalist Violet Blue wrote at the time, that *guy* was Clarence Wooten, whom sold his company, ImageCafe, for millions in 1999, well before Arrington and TechCrunch were even known quantities.

But Wooten didn't pattern match.

Since then, the number of black founders has grown considerably. Still, though, we get less than two percent of Silicon Valley investment. And that's now. Not ten years ago.

Today, they call it "culture fit." You don't match the pattern of those of us already in the room, so we do not trust the worth you bring to the table. You don't seem to culturally identify with what we've experienced, so we do not see the value of your contribution.

The pendulum swings from explaining your reason for being to proving you actually belong in the room beyond the scope of other's limited view of you.

If you don't match the pattern, if you don't fit the culture, then you are paying a resource tax. It is invisible, pervasive, and constant. Like air.

When I say I bootstrapped my two startups (building them from scratch with no outside investment) and sold the second one at a profit, it means something different as a thirty-something African-American stay-at-home dad with two college degrees. I paid and still pay a resource tax – a cut taken right off the top, like FICA and Social Security – before I even show up. It is remaining focused as people who look just like me are killed in front of their children on camera, their soul trapped eternally in a hashtag. It is adapting as the opportunities for myself and people like me narrow within an increasingly corrupt system. It is maximizing time as I untie emotional trauma passed down from generation to generation, cleansing my soul of unconscious biases to not cap my own two black and brown sons. It is finding energy as I fight against what others believe are my limitations simply because of who I culturally am.

Chances are, your 24 hours a day are not the same as mine.

This is also why believing you can accomplish as much in 24 hours as any said celebrity will corrode you like rust. Rust cannot begin on the outside. Rust always starts on the inside. The crack in your own worth lets the productivity virus in. The compare and contrast will drive you into the ground.

Where our resources need to go matters as much as how many resources we need. It is pure mathematics: for the average American, making $100,000 annually would be enough for a comfortable life (the average American household brings in around $60,000). But what if you live in San Francisco, where, when I was there in the late aughts, I paid four-figures for a tiny studio? Or if you were plowing through hundreds of thousands of dollars of debt, where the interest alone would be your monthly take-home pay? Or if you had family, friends, and loved ones dependent on your paycheck because of systematic circumstances beyond their and your immediate control?

Money is the most tangible example, but, of course, I'm not really talking about money.

I'm talking about weight.

There is a mental, physical, and emotional weight we carry when we face an undiagnosed health issue, when we feel guilt for a taking a sorely-needed break because of required responsibilities, and when we struggle with not reaching our potential because of on our seemingly too limited resources.

But to give yourself grace, you first have to recognize the battle.

Systematic oppression hums along in the background like an air conditioner. It is on when you enter the room and, after an almost imperceptible adjustment, its buzzing in the background becomes the norm. (Now, imagine if you are born in the air-conditioned room.) You fight to block out the noise. You work twice as hard to progress half as far. You don't see this resource tax. You are just used to paying it.

But what if the air conditioning suddenly turns off, as it did for all of us in March 2020? We realize how loud we had been talking just to be heard, how distracting the noise had been to our focus, and how much long-term planning we gave away just to get through the day.

"As I make my suffering conscious, less is passed on to others," says spiritualist Chani Nicholas. "As I come to understand what was personal, what was systemic, and what was familial, I get closer to the truth; I am more than what hurts, but I am not above being taught by the process of pain relief."

We're angry at 2020, not because it is a bad year, but because it has woken many of us up from a long slumber. We realize how autocratic our democracy really can be. We realize the system will automatically continue to chew up and spit out black and brown lives, even as we sleep peacefully in our own homes. We realize how quickly our financial security can be shredded to pieces, as if we're sitting in the low end of a soup bowl.

We realize how long we've been fighting upstream every day. But the river isn't directed by nature, but by man.

Which means we can change it.

Salmon

By default, you bring your previous system with you to the next experience.

*Esther Perel,
Steal the Show with Michael Port*

We believe our personal GPS is broken. We don't trust it anymore.

We think we're asking for too much, when we have hardly been compensated enough. We feel like we're being extra or unreasonable fighting for basic rights, when others don't have to validate their existence at all. We feel like we just need to work harder, when we see others moving forward faster seemingly with ease.

We often move against our instincts even when, especially when, the world itself is upside down.

Women have been labeled naturally giving and self-sacrificing. This so-called compliment sets the expectation that they should be happy to put themselves last, not have their needs fulfilled, and accept having their credit taken for brilliant ideas.

It isn't a mistake: white women still make 78 cents on the dollar compared to white men in the same job, and black and brown women are closer to half a dollar to that same dollar. That resource tax is passed on to the very corporations that employ them. Literally pennies paid on the dollar.

The LGBTQ community may get married, but doesn't have the rights to have anal sex in many states, even if it may be a part of adult intimacy. Black people may legally have a gun permit, but will still get shot by the police for having a firearm, as Minnesotan Philando Castile was in front of his young daughter in 2016.

We are traveling upstream. Even when we lean in, even when we follow the rules, even when we are being a "good citizen." Even when we are told and believe that we'll do better when we do better.

We are traveling upstream simply based on who we are.

The secret is we may be more prepared to nourish the world than the dominating voices.

You are ready for the more equitable world. This has all been training for you to usher it in.

"We have to look at it with the mindset that we're equal. Shit, we're not only equal, but we had to live at the bottom. There are parts of us that are superior because we've had to live underwater damn near and we can hold our breath longer than you," comedian Chris Rock said on *The Daily Show*.

I come from a long line of hustlers. My father as well as my stepfather (whom I call

Pop) are freelancers and entrepreneurs, as is my closest uncle. My Pop's dad was an entrepreneur, too. But my grandfather never subscribed to *Inc. Magazine*, my father never sat me down to talk independence, nor did my stepfather say he was an entrepreneur. As I share in *Bring Your Worth*, "Not one of my African-American predecessors called themselves an entrepreneur. I don't recall ever hearing it come out of my family's mouth." No, my grandfather, born in North Carolina in the thirties, began opening his own speakeasies likely because he and his people weren't comfortable, or even welcome, in the white bars. My father became an independent artist after he realized corporations would steal his ideas while simultaneously downplaying his contribution in ways not seen with his counterparts. My Pop launched his own mortgage company when he accepted that his white partners would never share equity based on his work.

They discovered the resource tax – the bifurcated focus between who they were and how they were perceived, the adapting from their cultural needs to conforming just to operate in mainstream white America, the time spent building their own insights and proving why it matters to those in charge, and the energy being true to their vision while being blocked from expressing it. It was an additional layer of friction, a resource tax they ponied up as soon as they showed up as themselves.

And, one day, they decided to stop paying it.

The cost were conditional relationships, perceived security, and stable money. The reward was freedom.

Award-winning filmmaker Ava DuVarnay put it like this: "My truth is I don't want a chair at the table. Or even three or even half anymore. I want the table rebuilt. In my likeness. And in the likeness of others long forced out of the room."

We go upstream because we are fighting for a seat at the table. We go upstream because we want validation. We go upstream because we want to blend in.

But you weren't meant to blend in. You were meant to rebuild. Otherwise, why are you here?

"Sometimes it gets exhausting. Sometimes it doesn't feel fair. But the idea that you would just stop and give up is something that would be a betrayal to our ancestors." Barack Obama said in a recent interview. "The sacrifices [our ancestors] made did, in fact, make a difference. There is greater power, greater freedom, greater representation. This idea that somehow no progress has been made is mistaken. So, we have an obligation to do all the work now to make sure that our grandkids fifty years from now, they look back and they say, 'Y'all had to put up with that?' And the reason they won't is because we did the work."

We can have intense, often overwhelming clarity on the work ahead, but it can take us a while to recognize the work done by our predecessors before we got here. Like a child discovering something new and believing she is the first to find it, we don't always see that people have walked the path we're on. They may have made our path clearer. Without them, the path may not even exist.

As I share in *Bring Your Worth*, it took me decades to realize my lineage "planted seeds in me, watching each and every one struggle and beam and fight and declare themselves, through action and persistence and vision, saying 'I'm here to make my mark'. These ideas, like me knowing what to charge the market for my services, or being able to negotiate based on some seemingly invisible service I provide, or even me knowing the value of what I bring to a world that isn't ready for it today, but will be ready for it tomorrow, I do not and cannot take full credit for that. I watched them, just like you watched others. "

"When a young person tells his parents, 'This is my body; this is my life. I can do what I want with it' he is only partly right,' Buddhist monk Thich Nhat Hanh says in *No Mud, No Lotus*. 'He doesn't see that he is a continuation of his parents and of his ancestor before that. This body is not yours alone. It is also the body of your ancestors. Your body is a collective product of your nation, of your people, of your culture, of your ancestors. So you are not strictly an individual. You are partly collective... Even if you don't have a regular interpersonal relationship with your parents or your ancestors, your body and mind contain their suffering and their hopes as well as your own," Thich Nhat Hanh says in *No Mud, No Lotus*.

If you do not fit the straight old white male norm, then you are essentially multilingual. The more culture norms from which you deviate, the more languages you know. (In my community we call it "code switching", or using different words and dialects based on the culture you're trying to navigate. Proper English in the boardroom, while casual slang among friends.) These dimensions reflect your potential cultural impact. They are like sides of a die, different parts of your cultural depth, but all represented at once, and all representing you. And, just like my long-dormant New Jersey accent surfacing whenever I get excited, they are ever present. You bring your blackness to work. You take your queerness into every business relationship. You carry the femininity or masculinity you identify with into every room. It doesn't matter if other people acknowledge, identify, or respect it. This richness creates an abundance of insight, a well of strength, and a security of identity unavailable from the outside world. To paraphrase Julia Cameron, it is your vein of gold.

Mainstream America suffers because these other dimensions are being undervalued, underfunded, and otherwise dismissed. As DuVarney says, leadership has succeeded in keeping diverse voices from having a seat at the table. While living in Silicon Valley, my close friends, colleagues, and associates bootstrapped YouTube, Dropbox, and other companies that would eventually change the world. Before 2005, independent creators could not build their own following and needed to appease gatekeepers on the radio or on the television. Before 2008, it was impossible to do your hard work on one device and seamlessly keep doing work on another device, and now you could create without being tethered to a laptop, an office, or even a continent. But I was there: the establishment initially thought their ideas were crazy, or unrealistic, or impractical. The people at the table couldn't read the cultural vision. The cosigns from companies like Google, or the support from startup accelerators like Y-Combinator, would come well after they created power from their own viewpoint. In their own image. In other words, they shifted the point of power by building from now. They were the vanguard.

But more than a decade later, those investments and that support have become even scarcer. Most Silicon Valley-funded startups are led by white male founders, followed by Asian males.

Their pattern matching worked. Their culture fit is accurate. But it comes at what cost?

In Summer 2020, Donald Trump signed an executive order to ban TikTok. The short-video app had grown exponentially in users within a few short years. Facebook, LinkedIn, and Instagram started cloning its bite-sized content strategy, to the point where TikTok users would just slap their content onto Instagram – TikTok logo in the corner and all. It was so powerful, TikTokers systematically organized to buy free tickets to Trump's Oklahoma City rally – and then didn't show up, leaving potentially thousands of seats empty. The rally was a bust. Within a week, Trump said the app needed to be banned.

What was Trump's argument? The most powerful app in recent memory was not made in Silicon Valley. It was made in China.

What happened to the innovation? In America, everyone in power is looking at the same side of the die. It is the equivalent of neighborhood gentrification: the counterculture makes something out of nothing, the hipper mainstream kids pick up on it and share it with the masses, the masses absorb this cultural vision while intentionally or unintentionally pricing the counterculture out.

The price could be access to capital to make the vision real, the price could be being privileged enough to not have your contributions undervalued, the price could be being allowed to move forward because of the color of your skin, whom you prefer to sleep with, or where you are from.

And once the pattern matching is complete, and the cultural fit is executed, then the new leaders wonder where the magic went. Remember when this neighborhood was gritty? Remember when it had flavor? Remember the soul it had? They don't realize that the magic is in the diversity.

"We are culture," Jay-Z says. "Nothing moves without us."

What Jay-Z is saying, what DuVarnay is saying, what established creative are saying, is that we have the special sauce. We can and should be creating our own table. Technology affords us the power to share our music with the world *for free*, to telegraph our vision live to the entire planet *for free*, and to establish our own worth with our own community *for free*.

They don't have anything for us but a co-sign from a dying worldview.

Eventually, they will understand the power of your cultural capital. It may happen today. It may happen later in your career. It may happen well after you are dead.

Waiting for validation is a fool's errand, though. For every Watson and Crick, there stands a Rosalind Franklin. For every Jack Daniels, there is an Uncle Nearest. For every person, institution, or system that holds the validation you seek, there is an individual who gave their cultural capital to it and was simultaneously absorbed into and erased by them. Because on some level they immediately recognize and are afraid of your power. It is like a pig being eager to get to the slaughter so their value will finally be validated.

"Everyone has a voice in their head, and every one of those voices is different," Godin says in *The Practice*. "Our experiences and dreams and fears are unique, and we shape the discourse by allowing those ideas to be shared. It might not work. But only you have your distinct voice, and hoarding it is toxic."

When we wait for the mainstream co-sign – the nod from a major influencer, the backing of an established entity, the acceptance into an exclusive club - and don't get it, it's not just depriving the culture at large. It is toxic to ourselves when we don't share it.

We automatically devalue our worth when we don't stand on our own.

"This wanting to be part of something, though, is bullshit," Chris Rock says. "Jackie Robinson got to play baseball, that's a great thing? No, those motherfuckers got to play with *him*! And you realize, when Jackie Robinson got to play baseball, it destroyed the Negro League – some of the only Black businessmen who were making real capital at the time. [It's about] having a stake in your own future."

You may ask yourself why you are so tired. For many of us, we have been creating what fashion icon Dapper Dan calls a parallel universe. The eighties legend handmade clothes worn by Mike Tyson, LL Cool J, and other New York elite by sewing together bootleg logos fashionable at the time. At his peak, Dapper Dan was raided, sued, and shut down. In a recent interview, he said traditional fashion business avenues weren't available to him.

"I entered the industry through retailing, but they denied me the right to buy luxury goods to sell. So I had no alternative, but to be creative on my own. I took a look at how we addressed this matter in history. So what I created was an 'alternative parallel universe'. If I can't be in their universe, I [will] create a universe of my own."

Decades later, in 2017, Dapper Dan was brought in to launch a fashion line – for Gucci. Their reputation wasn't as cool as it once was. It needed a boost.

We have to contribute, whether we bring our worth to the current systems or, as myself and my ancestors before me have done, create our own systems in our own likeness. As technology grows and the world gets smaller, we have more opportunities to do the latter than ever in history.

"Whenever I speak to young guy or gals with this frustration, what I say to them is, 'Don't let the frustration turn into cynicism where you just think nothing can change.' Because the truth is, things have changed. It's just that it's an ongoing battle. It is not just a one-shot deal where you kind of climb the mountain and you just stay there," Barack Obama said in an interview. "The roots of racism in this country are deep, the psychology of it has lessened, but it never fully went away, the legacy of slavery and Jim Crow means that we started the race behind with respect to the resources in our communities, the way the criminal justice system was set up, the lack of representation in corporate America. All those things didn't just go away: They built up over 400 years, and they weren't just going to go away in just 50 years, let's say, my lifetime. You can expect that each time we took two steps forward, there was going to be some pushback, because there are forces within our society that don't want to give up status and privilege. They don't want a level playing field. By the way, that's not just true for African Americans."

"Not just true for African-Americans" means people of color, folks in the LGBTQ community, the neurodiverse, and the physically different. It is anyone who can check a box that represents "Other". But now, more than ever, being the "Other" is becoming the norm. Which means your voice is necessary to represent not just you, but others within your distinct community.

Bringing your worth means recognizing that, under the veneer of toxic capitalism and xenophobic myopia, your power is equal to their power, and that everything is a partnership. It means not waiting for permission to envision, create, and nourish the world, especially when others don't see it, as that vision initially belongs only to you. And it means knowing that your fight against racism, sexism, and other isms, has turned you and your people, with you and before you, more focused, agile, efficient, and resilient, in ways that you would be remiss to not honor. If anything, the suppressions of the past have only better prepared you to lead in the future. And the future is now.

This is true even for some of the people holding on to the edifice of power. Staying in the room often means showing only the parts of you that match the culture. Keeping your seat of power usually means you aren't bringing your whole self to the table. Your privilege can become your cage. It's ultimately up to you to set yourself free.

"It was up to me to toil that soil, and that process begins with even recognizing that the seeds are there," I say in *Bring Your Worth*.

Externally, you can reach your audience, make your own money, and bring your own worth.

The first battleground, though, remains an internal one.

Your System is the Lock and the Key

One dollar from your own system is worth a thousand dollars of another man's system.

*John Henry,
Earn Your Leisure Podcast*

Shame and guilt often walk hand-in-hand with your output of the day, the hour, or even the minute. To paraphrase Brene Brown, shame is when you feel like you aren't meeting the expectations of others, while guilt is when you feel like you aren't meeting the expectations of yourself. Both are intertwined, as you can internalize society's expectations of you and take it on as your own.

It wasn't always this way. For centuries, the main measurement of your worth was how your craft provided for yourself and your family. The concept of hustling every day wasn't a badge of honor – it was just something everyone did. The axiom "I'll sleep when I'm dead" wasn't a point of pride. If you were an early-to-rise farmer, hard-working craftsperson, or what in modern terms we'd call a day laborer, then you didn't have much time to sleep anyway.

You just did your job based on the resources you had at the moment.

Our biggest hurdle today isn't finding the right hack to more output, but realizing that accepting our limitations actually improves our results.

Years ago, my family and I went to Italy and ate our way through several cities, each meal seemingly better than the last. The food tasted both simple and rich. When we asked about the meal, even at most humble location, they would unfailingly say that the pasta was made in house, the wine harvested from the next door neighbor's vineyard, the fish caught by the locals this morning, and so on. It was odd coming back home, going out in our charming San Diego neighborhood, and paying a premium to have what we Americans call the "farm-to-table" experience. It was strange because we were paying extra to have an establishment maximize our experience with the local resources at the moment. Why does nearly every Venetian restaurant serve squid? Because Venice is surrounded by water. It is also why they don't serve a lot of chicken or beef. The restaurateurs respect their offerings and, because of the limitations, actually master the resources' they've got, honoring both the land and the customers they serve.

In conversations with hundreds, if not thousands of creatives over the years, I see many of us landlocked looking for fish. It is the new parent trying to find time to be creative. It is the senior citizen pushing to do all-nighters. It is the 9-to-5-ers believing the only way they'll have the energy to pursue their dream is to immediately quit the day job. We are not honoring where we are, who we are, and what we've got in this moment.

The problem is we mistake productivity, which is one of the most loaded words in modern history, with effectiveness, which is based on your own particular goals, resources, and abilities.

On productivity, the word has been redefined in ways that don't fit strong personal health, well being, or even output. It wasn't always this way. As recently as 2016, I published *The Productive Bite-Sized Entrepreneur*, on how you can maximize your time without burning yourself out. The operative word here is "your." Not how you can maximize the organization's time, the government's time or, more broadly, society's time. Your time. Being productive should be based on your own criteria. Thus, the personal productivity goals and expectations of, say, a 75-year-old retiree will likely be different than that of a 25-year-old grad student. Unfortunately, society's ruler of measurement is often the same. Check the ever-popular magazine cover stories featuring the next young, sort-of-proven entrepreneurial prodigy – like the now-disgraced Theranos founder Elizabeth Holmes – or celebrating how much venture capitalist money a startup got – even though, to paraphrase Shark Tank investor Mark Cuban says, you are essentially leveraging against your future.

"There are plenty of '30 Under 30' lists. I recommend '40 Over 40' and '50 Over 50.' And when we do that, let's celebrate the older people who are working and the older people who aren't working. Showcase this amazing talent that can then be hired instantly," says 60-year-old Make Love Not Porn founder Cindy Gallop. An ad industry veteran, Gallop wants us to question why we hold certain metrics dear and totally disregard others. "If you're told that the target is youth and millennials, ask why. My industry plays a powerful role in shaping the way people think and behave. Here is a way we can use this power for good. When we make age aspirational in advertising, we make age aspirational in real life."

The fact is your strengths – the powers you draw on to be an effective leader, citizen, or creator – will change depending on your circumstances. These changes can be slow, or these changes can be rapid. They are based on where you are in your life.

Our lives are like the grooves of a vinyl record. They begin smooth and impressionable, like a black acetate. Over time, the feedback of our environment and the call of our needs create habits. The needle falls into the groove, making the patterns more ingrained. Even when we direct the needle elsewhere, it naturally falls from the peak into the comfortable valley.

What we often forget is that our best grooves are everchanging. These grooves are animated, ebbing and flowing based on where we are and who we are. They are far from static. They are alive.

I call them the F.A.T.E.s: Focus, Agility, Time, and Energy. These resources are our life force, neverending until we end. They are life itself.

Anthropomorphizing them helps us realize that they, truly, are not under our control. If you are hoping to will yourself to have incredible Focus, to become super Agile, to make more TIME, or to have unstoppable ENERGY, then I have some bad news for you! Just as an octogenarian, no matter how fit, cannot match the ENERGY of a healthy teenager, we should not expect to will our best resources into some pretzel knot of power. In fact, most of our power gets wasted in trying to either utilize the same resource – or FATE – we had in abundance before that we no longer have now, or to make ourselves master a resource we have very little of now in hopes of it becoming our main resource tomorrow.

This remains wishful thinking at best.

Instead, you can look at these resources like levers: they aren't absolutes, and they operate independently of each other. You may have a brief period where all four are at their peak. More often, though, one trait will run be particularly high and at least one particularly low.

Mastery isn't about keeping all four at their peak. This thinking is unrealistic, if not unhealthy. For example, surviving a serious health procedure or trauma and immediately pushing to maximize your ENERGY doesn't make much sense at all. You need space to heal, so perhaps TIME becomes one of your activated powers.

Instead, the goal here is to maximize whatever phase you are in your life. Each lever possesses its own different strengths and attributes.

If you are hyper-FOCUSED, then your view should be on big picture thinking. It's possible to be so myopic that you succeed at one narrow goal, but you miss out on the bigger win.

If you are super AGILE, then you should hone your consistency. Being flexible can become a weakness without having a set plan or commitment.

If you have ample TIME, then your main challenge is, as business leader Adam Grant calls it, attention management. The more TIME you have, the bigger danger you have of wasting it.

Lastly, if you have an abundance of ENERGY, then your main challenge is goal management. It is easy to waste plenty of ENERGY pursuing the wrong milestone.

Perhaps the biggest challenge in understanding your strengths is acknowledging what you *don't* have in your toolbox. This requires vulnerability. You may not have the ENERGY to help someone move their furniture or to help them fight their fight, but you might have the time to listen to them and give them the encouragement they need to fight that fight or to just move that furniture. You might not be able to physically be at an event for them because of previous commitments, but you can show up in another important room entirely and make sure their name is mentioned. You could miss the opportunity to be for someone at that moment, but you can show them in other ways that you care as much as do. You may not be able to take on their burden, but you can connect them with someone else who may help carry the load. It is being vulnerable enough to say, "I can't do that," or "It is not possible." It is learning to say "No".

When we show up no matter what, then deny our emotional, physical, and mental boundaries, and we go going upstream when we really should be acknowledging our current moment. The ego gets involved when we worry about our limitations: we're having a hard time focusing, so we beat ourselves up about procrastination, or circumstances give us a blank slate to work with, and we get mad about not being sure what to do with the sudden time we have on our hands. Instead, we have the opportunity to recognize our versatile, curious mind of the moment, or to honor our rare chance to do things at our own pace. But first, we have to understand, acknowledge, and accept our boundaries of the moment.

If you do happen to be hyper-Focused, super Agile, Time abundant, and extra Energetic at the moment, then that balance will likely last for quite literally that: a moment. Balance doesn't mean all cylinders going. Balance means knowing the strengths of your current life, embracing your place, and leaning into your flow. Balance means your abundance parallels your lack, and knowing that the cycle can and will change in the future based on the past. Balance means creating where you naturally rise, like a river automatically finding the subtle cracks in the basin created before the drought. You don't worry about the strengths you don't have for the moment, as you know, as long as you breathe, life can shift at any time and change where your abundance lies.

"There are people and organizations in our lives that we trust. How did that happen? We develop trust over time," Seth Godin says in *The Practice*. "Our interactions lead to expectations, and those expectations, repeated and supported, turn into trust. These organizations and people earn trust by coming through in the difficult moments. They're not perfect; in fact, the way they deal with imperfection is precisely why we trust them. We can do the same thing to (and with) ourselves. As we engage in the practice, we begin to trust the practice. Not that it will produce the desired outcome each time, but simply that it's our best available option. Trust earns you patience, because once you trust yourself, you can stick with a practice that most people can't handle."

Your purpose isn't to make things happen. Your purpose is to recognize the best timing to create. Part of that timing is based on how you create in the first place.

Your current strengths represent this timing. Your current strengths represent the fates.

Here's how you can embrace them.

UNDERSTANDING THE FATES

According to the creation story in the biblical book of Genesis, God said, "Let there be light." I like to imagine that light replied, saying "God, I have to wait for my twin brother, darkness, to be with me. I can't be there without the darkness." God asked, "Why do you need to wait? Darkness is there." Light answered, "In that case, then I am also already there."

Thich Nhat Hanh,
No Mud, No Lotus

In my research, I've found the very ways to maximize your biggest resources also match how you can best compensate for your lowest resources. For instance, if you have an abundance of TIME, then you can maximize it by setting clear, definitive boundaries and strong, strategic goal setting. How do you handle things when TIME is scarce? Set clear, definitive boundaries and do strong, strategic goal setting. As Wharton professor Adam Grant says, it's not about time management, but attention management, and we can use that whether we have a bunch of time or not much time to spare. They present different sides of the same coin.

Some guidance books recommend taking the knowledge specific to you and reading that chapter. This isn't one of those books. In fact, that would be a mistake. Your resources aren't monolithic.

We all have the ability to FOCUS, to be AGILE, to maximize TIME, and to use ENERGY. We do until the day we die. So each one of these resources are immediately relevant to you. They all are. Stories, examples, analogies, and contrasts between the different resources are woven throughout.

My recommendation? Read the book, *then* do the quiz in the back of the book or, even better, online at www.buildfromnowquiz.com. You'll be able to get a feel for different resources, which is important because your primary resource today is based on personal and professional circumstances that will likely change tomorrow. Remember, your resources are not fixed. If you take the quiz post-reading, you could be pleasantly surprised, too.

The veil between you and your subconscious self thin when you have an intense, life-relevant experience. A messy divorce, a painful funeral, or a child's birth don't automatically cause reinvention; two people may have the same experience, but one may seem unchanged, while the other utterly transformed.

Usually, though, the veil is too thick for us to be objective. Through reading this, I want us to slow down enough to see the patterns, feel the pain, and respect our past and present enough to acknowledge our best strengths and limitations.

Your dominant resource represents what classic business theorist Chris Argyris calls your Ladder of Influence.

We go through five steps when we get new information:
- we select the data relevant to us;

- we paraphrase the data in language we understand;
- we label the data to describe what we believe is happening;
- we explain or evaluable what's happening;
- and we decide what to do.

Then we do it.

This would be less important if we looked at every experience in a fresh light. But we don't. We begin to see what we believe and experience things in ways that confirm the world to be.

This phenomenon plays into our FATEs. It is why we will keep doing all-nighters (ENERGY as our primary resource) even though we're way past a point in our life when it makes sense; It may be more efficient and comfortable stretching the deadline (TIME as our primary resource), but we're locked in the habit.

There are a few things at work here.

First, we have "confirmation bias", which means we're more likely to accept data that fits our world view and, frankly, our ego. We like *feeling* right more than actually *being* right. It gives us security. "We have millions of questions that need answers because there are so many things that the reasoning mind cannot explain. It is not important if the answer is correct; just the answer itself makes us feel safe. This is why we make assumptions," Don Miguel Ruiz says in *The Four Agreements*.

We can be so eager to create a narrative, we tell ourselves a story and commit to it before we even have all the important details. In *Rising Strong*, Brene Brown says about how storytelling could also be our downfall: "We're wired for story and in the absence of data we will rely on confabulations and conspiracies.... More information means less fear-based story-making." Filling in the blanks gives us comfort, not clarity.

Second, the more you think about something, the more likely you'll see it. For instance, if you worry about your ability to maximize your Time, then you're more likely to be paralyzed when you have to decide what to do with it – and then end up wasting your Time, confirming your own theory. Theorists call it the Baader-Meinhof phenomenon. (Pop culturalists call it The Streisand Theory, named after the singer who sued to get pictures of her secluded mansion off the web – and ended up drawing attention to pictures of her secluded mansion on the web.)

I talk about the Baader-Meinhof/Streisand trap in *The Ultimate Bite-Sized Entrepreneur*.

And we can totally Streisand our flaws: Focus on your weaknesses and you will see more and more of your flaws in your work and your life. Unfortunately, this will make you more likely to beat yourself up for minor mistakes and you may even emphasize your weak spots to potential coworkers or clients rather than highlighting your capabilities. There is little constructive that can come from blowing up your issues – and there's nothing you can do with the little information gained.

Third, Argyris' Ladder of Inference theory is the equivalent of an online "filter bubble", as your options begin to feel narrower and narrower because the framework is built to give you more of the same. Your mind works like a modern Internet browser, website, or social media platform: You liked this message from McDonalds? Well, let's show you an ad from Burger King, Wendy's and Jack In The Box. You bought this crib? Well, let's suggest you buy baby bottles, rompers, and a car seat.

And you like being AGILE? Makes you feel at your best? Feeds your ego, too? Well, we'll keep putting you in situations where you have to adjust at the last minute. Let's keep you feeling good.

The Ladder of Inference calls it a "reflexive loop" and it can have you leaning on a particular resource for unhealthy reasons:

Our assumptions, values, and beliefs influence how we select data, interpret what is happening, and decide what to do. Our interpretations and decisions then feedback to reinforce (usually) our assumptions, values, and beliefs. We act on the basis of our interpretations, and our actions affect what data is available to us. So our ways of understanding and acting in the world create a self-reinforcing system, insulating us from alternative ways of understanding.

As you look into your resources, do not believe one particular strength is the answer. Focus, Agility, Time, and Energy are all necessary for you to make any sort of impact on the world.

More importantly, partnering and respecting the different dimensions of you – of all of us – raises the bar for all. If you lean into Focus, then you will be totally sure when you have to be Agile, make the most of your Time, and have your Energy be concentrated on only the most important goals. If you embrace AGILITY, then you won't FOCUS on ideas that no longer serve you, be less likely to waste TIME mourning the past, and know quickly what goals give you the most ENERGY. If you understand TIME, then you can FOCUS on the long-term, be AGILE enough to adjust to the culture, and build disciplined, consistent ENERGY. And if you respect ENERGY, then you can bring serious FOCUS, keep your passion even as you are AGILE, and make the biggest impact with your TIME.

You have a dominant resource, but it is never your only resource.

Your resource is the filter to your world. As the saying goes, if you have a hammer, then everything is a nail. But the most dangerous thing is not knowing you're using a hammer at all.

II
AN INSIDE JOB

How to Partner with Focus

Your power is not measured by how many opportunities you can get. Your power is measured by what you have the ability to turn down... You have so much power, that [the opportunity] doesn't make sense to you.

Julian Mitchell,
The Business Behind Music and Culture
with John Henry

My dad left when I was very young: no doubt in part because both my parents were very young. As a career-driven new adult, my father told me later he wanted to establish himself first to properly provide for my mom and me (in retrospect, a very 22-year-old idea to believe). Of course, time waits for no man. My parents never reconciled, however cordial they remain. When I became a young man, I met the love of my life, courted her for several years, then got married and immediately had our first son – and launched my first startup at the same time. I was proving to myself that I could have a robust career and a healthy relationship with my own son. When I finally got to the TED stage, it was a talk about giving people – specifically children – attention. Overlaying my current FATE framework onto the past, my primary resource has almost always been focus.

That's because I believe focus is love. Giving something or someone your full attention changes it. I see it in my one-on-one coaching, looking my client right in the eye and letting them know we are on the journey together or holding on to one of my sons, afraid at the moment, and consciously calming my heartbeat so his will follow suit. My very ability to be highly driven, relentlessly strategic, and purposefully creating and needing intense connections to others is the result of my trauma.

These are the grooves in my vinyl record.

It's taken me years to not wear it as a badge of honor, saying that pain made me, or to argue that my childhood environment has nothing to do with the way I use resources today, plugging into some perverse, self-made man myth.

Instead, it just is. That, in itself, is freedom. That, in itself, is love. Self love.

Gameplan for Your Focus

1. Show up with one goal in mind
2. Constantly remember your intention
3. Remember why you do, not just what you do

How to Strengthen Your Focus

1. As soon as you wake up, write down your number one priority for the day
2. Do not immediately say "Yes", but politely give yourself time to consider what it requires
3. Think about what you want to accomplish next and the singular action that will get you closer

Boundaries for Your Focus

1. Create clear metrics on what you want
2. Establish early what you will or won't do to see the desired results
3. Check in often to make sure your idea, belief, or goal still serves you

FOCUS is nothing more than a decision. It is giving one solitary fuck, and making that fuck your objective at a specific moment.

FOCUS is not obsession. Obsessions are unconscious and, often, are the rooted in the avoidance of something else. Focus is not passion. As I wrote in *The Bite-Sized Entrepreneur*, "The truth is that passion will not get you out of bed every morning. Like love, it can be fickle and moody and fairweather." And FOCUS is not willpower. "The problem is that will and resources can never be equally prioritized," Simon Sinek says in *The Infinite Game*. "There are always circumstances in which one is pitted against the other."

FOCUS-rich individuals are not necessarily obsessed, passionate, or willful, just as FOCUS-low individuals cannot obsess, emote, or will their way to more FOCUS.

Focus is the act of consciously showing up at this very moment as well as you can. Being Focus-rich means choosing to show up again and again and again.

Award-winning author Ta-Nehisi Coates explains it this way: "It's not really that mystical. It's just repeated practice over and over again, and then suddenly you become something that you didn't realize you could really be. Or you just quit the field and realize you really suck (laughs). But hopefully, you have a breakthrough!"

But, how do you define 'breakthrough'? We can become too dependent or independent of Focus when we do not define our success. It is realistically navigating the gap between where you are and where you want to be, and what concentration it will take to get there.

Focusing on the process, Elizabeth Gilbert says, protects us from the extreme emotions of failure and success. "My point is that I'm writing another one now, and I'll write another book after that and another and another and another and many of them will fail, and some of them might succeed, but I will always be safe from the random hurricanes of outcome as long as I never forget where I rightfully live. Look, I don't know where you rightfully live, but I know that there's something in this world that you love more than you love yourself. Something worthy, by the way, so addiction and infatuation don't count, because we all know that those are not safe places to live. Right? The only trick is that you've got to identify the best, worthiest thing that you love most, and then build your house right on top of it and don't budge from it."

"There are three simple ways you can make [a change in the world] with more focus, energy, and success," Seth Godin says in *The Practice*. "First, you can embrace the fact that you can, in fact, trust the process and repeat the practice often enough to get unstuck. Second, you can focus on the few, not everyone. And third, you can bring intention to your work, making every step along the way count."

When my clients say, "I'm having a hard time focusing on this thing I really want," it really means they have at least one of three factors:

- Vague metrics of what they want; or
- Hidden assumptions about what they will or won't do to see the desired results
- Holding on to an idea, belief, or goal that no longer serves them

Ironically, it is also the very same factors when clients say, "I'm having a hard time letting this failing project go." Again, it is a trend I've seen in with folks having a surplus or a deficit of a particular resource: they can be in opposite situations with the same challenge.

First, what is the result you want?

If you're looking to get full, then it doesn't matter about the quality, health, or sustainability of the food. If you're looking to have a gourmet experience, then it may not matter how much it costs or how long you have to wait for the opportunity. We can expect to do a getting-full effort and unconsciously expect gourmet experience results. If you are Focus-rich, then you could be barking up the wrong tree and become increasingly frustrated with the progress. If you are Focus-challenged, then you could break your Focus quickly because you were expecting better results sooner.

Partnering with Focus means putting perfection on the shelf. Perfect is an ideal, not a goal.

I explain why in my 2018 TEDxToledo Talk, "Why You Should Strive for Good Enough":

Emotional intelligence pioneer Brene Brown says "Perfectionism is armor." It is different than an internal metric or standard that we have, as in 'I'll be better tomorrow than I am today.' That's good! That's growth. That's the way it's supposed to be. No, when you get into the perfectionist's mindset, it has nothing to do with internal; it is all external. And everything you do comes down to the same basic question: "But what will they think?"

Capital "T" in "They". "Perfectionism," Brene Brown says, "is our way of hiding our true selves."

You can't focus on being perfect because it doesn't exist. That's why striving for perfection remains good for only one thing: burnout.

Knowing what you want, though, is entirely different. It is tuning out the noise and stating your intention as clearly and plainly as possible.

To contrast, AGILITY is utilizing and maximizing whatever is in front of you. FOCUS is removing and minimizing nonessential things around you.

It is taking a magnifying glass and concentrating the sunlight – your attention – on a specific spot. The sun could have been beating that same spot all day, but now that concentration is organized, uniform, and exclusionary. It is easy to forget that you, the chair in which you sit, and every single thing around you is made up of molecules. And even the most solid objects are constantly vibrating, however slowly. The higher the heat, the faster the molecules move. Our concentrated attention adds more heat.

Focus creates flexibility in an otherwise immobile situation. To FOCUS, we have to be still while others move. In stillness, we see the true, deeper dimensions of a situation. Only in FOCUS, in stillness, and in singularity, can we see the multitude of cadences around us.

Second, what will or won't you do to see your desired results? As Seth Godin says in *The Dip*: "Write down under what circumstances you're willing to quit." I launched my first startup, So Quotable, at the same time I became the primary caretaker to my 3-month-old, Alec. He was my priority. If bootstrapping my first company ever prevented me from feeding, caring, or otherwise guiding Alec, then I would quit. No questions asked. Financial sacrifices, mental stress, and intense daily routines left me undeterred, as I could ask every morning "Am I doing right by Alec and, by extension, my family?" and confidently say, "Yes."

We don't always have these conversations about expectations and sacrifice, probably because we don't think about it until we have to. Scarcity breeds clarity. It is why we suddenly become specific towards end of life, become efficient when we take care of children or our elders, and become financially thoughtful when we get our first paycheck. The truth is that we always have these leaks – these minor incongruences that eat at our Focus, our Agility, our Time, and our Energy – that become major misalignments as we continue on. Big life moments don't create the disparity. They just expose the issues we've had all along.

The late Stephen Covey's classic *First Things First* has my favorite Focus framework. The premise is simple: Your life has big rocks and little rocks. The size represents the importance and, essentially, what should be prioritized. They all have to fit into a jar. Pour the little rocks in first and you can get them all in the jar, but you won't be able to fit the big rocks in. Put the big rocks in first, though, and then the little rocks will naturally fall into the remaining space allotted.

Your rocks will evolve over time. My kids don't need me as much now. Alec was my big rock, and my fledging startups, So Quotable and Cuddlr, had to be squeezed within the space between. Today, Alec and his younger brother, Abhi, are old enough to be more independent. I have the space to do seven books in four years, build a healthy coaching practice, and do way more keynote talks. The rocks changed.

When I first started as an entrepreneur, a good friend said, perhaps, my family was my real startup: low resources, minimal TIME, and little guidance. It helped me accept that priorities would have to be juggled and to be realistic with what was possible. Realizing your true priority can be tough but, when you do, you can truly maximize how effective you are at the most important thing.

You can fit nearly everything in, if you take care of the most important stuff first.

Focus isn't just in your outward actions, but what is top of mind for you. It is remembering your intention within chaos, building connections as you rest, and working on your process to be ready for your next breakthrough. The results we desire often manifest internally before they create an external event.

Poet and Andrew W. Mellon Foundation president Elizabeth Alexander talks about how we can always be actively creating, even if our output fluctuates based on the season of our lives.

I would often send writing students to look at a retrospective of an artist's work [and] the thing that you learn is that there are fallow periods and there are incredibly generative periods. There are periods where you're trying to work an idea out so you're kind of stuck in a groove and there are periods when you have breakthroughs. If you look on the walls there will be years where there's nothing at all. And I think it's also really interesting when you learn about the lives of the artists and I think about this with women artists in particular. Where they, you know, had children in those years? What were the usually family forces or forces within the self. Were they in a depression? Were they struggling with their health? Or were they just, to use the fantastic expression that jazz musicians use, were they just woodshedding. Were they in the woodshed just working on their craft, biding their time, trying to work it out in private so that then they could come out – shazam – with something different and public?

"Woodshedding" is building towards tomorrow based on our intention today. You're still working, even if you aren't moving. Practice your instrument so you don't have to focus on the basics. Sharpen your vision so you can focus strictly on your execution later. And, most importantly, build your systems so you don't have to focus on correcting sloppy mistakes when the stakes are higher.

In my coaching, one of the biggest dangers I see is wishing for a future you aren't prepared for. We can be so focused on what's next, we become myopic on what we can improve and control today. You want your product featured by Oprah, but have you tightened up your manufacturing enough to handle a 100x demand? It's cool to envision being a busy life coach, but have you researched and determined how many clients you can realistically serve?

Manifesting a millionaire lifestyle by age 25 is fine, but how are you going to serve the world in a way where you can financially there – and what personal cost are you willing to pay?

The late motivational speaker Jim Rohn explains it simply, as I share in *The Ultimate Bite-Sized Entrepreneur*:

"You say, 'If I had a big organization, you know, I'd really run it with a strong hand and I'd be a fabulous leader. But I've only got a few (followers) and I don't know where they are.' See, that's not going to work. If you wish to preside over a lot... you have to be disciplined when the amounts are small." What Rohn is talking about is systems: A system to master your emotional intelligence so you can handle the power; a system to handle your relationships so your management can

scale; and a system to organize your resources so you can use them most effectively in high numbers. The thing is that those systems can most easily be put into place when the overhead is as low as the stakes. Ironically, as Rohn mentions, it's easy to not take the systems seriously when the rewards are weak, yet this is the very time you should be thinking about long-range goals.

"People tend to start with a business model and then become unhappy when their days are filled with tasks they don't enjoy," Paul Jarvis says in *Company of One*. "Instead of thinking, What product can I create? or What service can I offer?, [*Atomic Habits* author James Clear] believes that we should first think: What type of life do I want? And How do I want to spend my days? Then you can work backwards from there into a business model that allows you to create scalable systems to deliver your product to your audience."

These systems are built around our Focus. For instance, Andrew W. Mellon's Elizabeth Alexander says she thought, when she became a mother, her creative muse would leave. Instead, during the midnight breastfeedings, she'd envision poetic lines, scribbling them down with a spare hand. Her Focus as an artist didn't die; she just evolved the system in which she created.

She says, "Once I got old enough to start realizing that for every day of my life I would not rise with the dawn and write into the light and do that every day and thus there would be a book every other year. It just doesn't work like that. Things happen in life. There are stages. There are eras in life."

Lastly, are you holding on to an idea, belief, or goal that no longer serves you? Inertia is a hell of a drug. It is easier to keep our Focus on something we've outgrown than to find a new direction. It can feel like losing our identity, even though, like skin cells refreshing every seven years, we're in a constant state of perpetual growth, change, and evolution.

It reminds me of a long-shared Thanksgiving story I first heard from my mother. I later realized that other people heard a variant of it in their lives:

A couple is getting the Thanksgiving ham ready to put in the oven. Suddenly, one of them takes out a large knife and begins cutting off the end of the raw ham - a significant chunk of it. "What are you doing?" her partner asks. "I'm getting the ham ready to put in the oven." "No, I mean, why are you cutting the end off?" "That's how my mom taught me to cook it." "Why?" "Because... I don't know."

Now curious, she goes over to her mom's house. "Why do you cut the end off of the ham?" "Because that's how Nana does it."

Now both perplexed, they go over to the retirement home to visit the grandmother. "Nana, why do we cut the end off of the ham?" The grandma pauses, then a light comes on in her eyes. "Well, during our first Thanksgiving we didn't have much money, and it was a tiny kitchen with an even tinier oven, so the only way we could make our ham fit would be to..."

Even more to the point, spiritualist Jessica Dore recently shared a New York Native American story of the Icehouse. A witch puts a group of men into an icehouse to freeze them to death. She even included ice chairs to sit in when they inevitably get tired, pushing them even closer to their demise. Instead, the wise men dance and sing all night. The body heat begins to melt the house, making holes in the ceiling and, eventually, letting the sun in.

They are free.

"Icehouses come in many models, shapes and sizes. Some are internal monologues that run on loop, some are classical trainings or informal social conditionings, some are thought patterns so subtle you don't know they're there until one day someone looks you in the eyes and says hey, that's foolish what you're doing on account of some assumption you never bothered to question," Dore says.

The icehouse, she says, is "any place in life where you have chosen to siphon or partition off vital ENERGY in service of staying the same. Any place you've thrown up a barricade against pretty much the one truly un-interruptible thing in life, which is change." In other words, your FOCUS isn't on growth, but your FOCUS is on *not* growing. You can't hide and create at the same time. You can't be safe and improve simultaneously. You can't get there from here.

The word "siphon" is perfect here, as you're stealing FOCUS from potential future greatness and giving it to a past that no longer serves you or the world.

Think about the last time you spent an inordinate amount of TIME for an incremental improvement on a completed project. Now, imagine all the other things you could have been doing with that time. At a certain point, spending more TIME on something will provide significantly diminished returns. That inordinate amount of TIME can have devastating effects on your *big rocks*. It is better to ship it out, get it out the door, and move on to the next task, as having the perfect little rock won't help you manage any of your big rocks – assuming you have any room left for your true priorities.

In *Big Magic*, Elizabeth Gilbert talks about ideas leaving when they aren't acted upon:

What was the idea supposed to do, sit around indefinitely while I ignored it? Maybe. Sometimes they do wait. Some exceedingly patient ideas might wait years, or even decades, for your attention. But others won't, because each idea has a different nature. Would you sit around in a box for two years while your collaborator blew you off? Probably not. Thus, the neglected idea did what many self-respecting living entities would do in the same circumstances: It hit the road.

You could be holding on to the corpse of an idea already past its time. You're focusing on an empty husk. Windows of opportunity don't always close, but they do have a shelf life. What opportunities are you missing when you're focused on an expired idea?

"Locate your icehouses," Jessica Dore warns. "You'll know them because they are the places that what was once supple, flexible and teeming with life goes to do its hardening, stiffening and waiting around to die. Now ask yourself this: What dances can I do, *will I do*, what songs can I sing, *will I*, in order to revive those things, in order to keep them alive."

The proverbial dance is simple: Remembering the weight of a bad goal far outstrips any benefits of persistence. "What should I give up?" is as essential of a question as "What should I begin?"

There's a wonderful urban myth about veteran comedian Bill Murray. For years, it has been said that he'll pop up to a stranger, or no more than a few people, at a random, unassuming moment, do something just odd enough to get their attention, and then say, "You can tell others that Bill Murray did this, but no one will believe you." And then he'd leave as suddenly as he came. It would be a benign activity, like crashing a small, public wedding happening in the park, or dropping in on a young rock band playing loud in their apartment. Many of these events reportedly happened before cell phones were common and cheap; the onlookers couldn't just snap him and capture him in a viral video. The Saturday Night Live alum is known for his straight-face, sardonic comedy, and the improvised moments always seemed to be hilarious to the people involved. But, as he presumably predicted, when they'd share these funny incidents, no one else believed them.

In 2018, new director Tommy Avallone made a documentary about the nationwide phenomenon, *The Bill Murray Stories: Life Lessons Learned from a Mythical Man*. It all turns out to be true.

But what happens to people in the gap between their Bill Murray encounter on, say, a golf course in Biloxi, Mississippi, and that moment when Avallone's indie movie shows *everyone else* that they were telling the truth all along? Did they spend the TIME trying to convince others in their lives that it really happened? Did they quietly cherish the thought, like a childhood memory only you recall? Or, after meeting skepticism, did they eventually convince *themselves* that it never happened at all?

What you know to be true, what you value as a Focus, could be a little fuzzy around its definition or as clear as the Sun rising in the East. Honestly, it doesn't matter. What does matter is how much you depend on someone or something else to validate your truth. The more important the change in which you seek, the more pressure you will be under to trade your truth for another person's truth. It is never a fair trade.

Your work may be seasonal. Your intention is not.

How to Partner with Agility

We don't have a map, but what we do have is a compass. A map lays everything out for you. A compass says, "Go that way." ... It doesn't care what's in your way, and, if you're following this compass, neither do you.

*Chase Jarvis,
The Chase Jarvis Show, Creator Therapy
with Seth Godin in New York*

When my eldest son was young, he would get up in the middle of the night wide awake. I would want my wife to sleep, and, when we were at my in-laws house, not to disturb the rest of the household. So I'd put on my pants, search for my keys in the lightless house, and then grab him and hustle to the car in the dark.

Our summer baby must have been around 6-months-old, as I distinctly remember seeing my breath in the chilly California winter air. He may have fussed, but, once we started moving, everything would grow silent.

I remember the hallmark Southern California traffic would be virtually gone, aside from an occasional, fast-moving pickup truck or a slow driver with an out-of-state license plate. The stars would be clear and bright. I'd occasionally binge on a business podcast, as I was just getting into the pleasures of audio rather than reading – being a baby's primary caretaker means you can't just sit and read a book, as your hands have other immediate needs.

Often, though, it was just me, my thoughts, and the endless road. I imagined being a New York cab driver, an active participant in the scene, but still objective enough to appreciate the spectacle of the night, and tired from the time of day, but lucid enough to drive. It was like removing a filter from my emotional landscape. Odd memories from childhood, assumptions I suddenly realized were opinion, not fact, and new, seemingly obvious business ideas floated to the blank dashboard ahead.

It would happen anytime from 1 a.m. to 3 a.m., and, because he'd often wake up if I lifted him out, it wasn't unusual for me to drive until just before dawn. I'd come back tired, of course, but also invigorated, as if I'd taken a long, hot bath, or had an amazing post-coital moment. It was as if I discovered something that made everything clearer.

It took me many nights, though, to embrace this chaos. I remember being angry at my son for not sleeping, as if he were somehow doing it just to get under my skin or, perhaps, I was doing something wrong and was, despite my desire to love, just an ill-equipped father. I would feel bitter because it was my job to chauffeur him around, a job that no one else could do and a job that, when my wife and I decided to have a baby, I actually was stupid enough to elect to do. I sat salty, back sore from lack of sleep and arms tired from being at the 10 and 2, as I drove for hours with literally no particular place to go. I was being pulled in directions

I didn't want to be, physically and otherwise.

Once I began to accept this interruption, then I started to relax. As an introvert, I realized these one, two or three hours of silence could be part of how I recharged, like a bonus solitude away from the daily fatherhood ruckus. I began to lean into these moments and, when he fussed hard in the middle of the night, I'd embrace the challenge.

The white space is, by definition, uncomfortable. It is the time before a decision is made. It is the gap from the first action to the next action. It is often without a definitive end and, sometimes, without even a definitive beginning.

It is also a gift. Floating between here and there, the white space gives us the objectivity to see how we operate. It exposes our systems. It widens the moment between response and reaction, as it doesn't allow us to jump to the next conclusion, and if we do, our reaction just sits in space, like a vacuum, for us to see and digest.

This clarity is a rare opportunity. All things eventually conclude, even the moments when we are too distant to see the shore and too far to see the destination.

My son turned seven this summer. His younger brother just turned four. The endless road has ended. And that white space now is becoming a distant memory in itself.

Gameplan for Your Agility

1. Trust your curiosity
2. Lean into observing what's next
3. Believe every new experience will be useful later

How to Strengthen Your Agility

1. Let someone else take the lead in an area you usually control
2. Try making small changes in your habits to exercise your flexibility muscle
3. Learn a new hobby that will help you apply old concepts to new experiences

Boundaries for Your Agility

1. Adding more because we can
2. Believing something needs to be changed when it just needs to be persevered

Busta Rhymes is a quintessential New York rapper. In fact, many fans – including myself – would put him among the Top 10 rappers of all time.. He began his career in high school with the short-lived, influential hip-hop group Leaders of the New School. What keeps him top of mind as a solo artist, however, is consistent AGILITY: His breakout hit, 1995's "Woo-Haa!! Got You All in Check," has him rapping at a stream-of-conscious, dizzying clip; his 1997 landmark song "Put Your Hands Where My Eyes Can See" is him flowing almost ridiculously low and slow, as if he's trying to match the level of the deep syncopated bass drums; and one of his biggest appearances, on Chris Brown's 2011 club smash "Look at Me Now", is rapped so fast that there are viral videos of listeners – and fellow rappers – attempting to following his lines. (They often fail.)

Now a middle-aged rapper, Busta just released his tenth studio album. He started as a teenager in the late eighties.

On Drink Champs, a video podcast hosted by fellow veteran New York rapper N.O.R.E. and Miami DJ EFN, he explains what happens when he enters the recording booth.

On a deeper level, too, I don't think people realize how beautiful it is to be able to go into the studio as an artist and lock yourself into those four walls... You love your woman, you love your kids, your mom, your friends, everybody, but the studio don't argue with you. The studio don't ask you no questions. And the studio don't stress you out, bro... There's a lot of times when I go to the studio and I just sit there and I don't even create nothing. I just go in there for some peace of mind... but when I go in the studio, not only do I get the chance to avoid shit I don't want to be bothered with, but I can also become whomever I choose to be. If I think about becoming a fucking Avenger in the studio, I can become an Avenger. If I want to become The Incredible Hulk in the studio, I can be The Incredible Hulk. That's a fact. And you can freely share whatever those thoughts and feelings are and capture it. And there are no repercussions, because you can live with it for a week or two to determine whether or not you even want to share this shit. And the world doesn't have to give you criticism within that space of you trying to create it. And then you can go back and revisit it, and perfect it, and revisit it, and perfect it, and get it to a place where it is so impeccable that before you even share it a [playable] form, you've mastered the intricacies of this thing so phenomenally, you already know what it's going to be when they hear it, you already know what it's going to be on that stage, and you already know what it's going to be when it's time to compete.

AGILITY is play. You could do this. You could do that. The possibilities initially seem endless. When you show up in the arena, as Brene Brown might say, you don't know what mood you'll be in, what will be on your mind, or how your first action will land. It's like poker the moment right before you get your hand. And, like a card shark, Busta can anticipate how things may go ("You already know what it's going to be when they hear it, you already know what it's going to be on that stage, and you already know what it's going to be when it's time to compete.") because he's spent so much TIME in the arena. It's the same way I can envision how this book will land when I share it with my coaching clients, as I talk about it from a keynote stage, and, as we discuss in the Understanding Your FATEs chapter, where it sits among other creative business books.

But notice that Busta isn't just saying what he can do. These four walls. Outside voices aren't let in. There are restrictions and boundaries to this expression. This, in turn, gives him the freedom to explore. When you're anticipating that five-stud poker hand, you know you're not going to get an UNO card. You know anything you get will be an Ace, a King, or something in between. Anything else would be shocking. Anything else would make you question fully exploring the possibilities. Anything else would make you feel unsafe to play.

The boundaries make us free.

Timing is different than TIME. As a resource, TIME is maximizing the literal moments you've got to make the greatest positive impact. AGILITY is timing: knowing when to move and, since the best opportunities usually don't give much notice, it about always being prepared.

AGILITY is trusting yourself to make the next best move. It is intuitive, fluid, and welcoming.

In her book *The Creative Leap: Unleash Curiosity, Improvisation, and Intuition at Work*, consultant Natalie Nixon describes the intuitive process in three steps:

Think of leading with intuition as three concentric circles. Wonder is at the core because stillness and observation are required for us to hear that little voice inside. The second circle is discernment – finding the strength to act on our intuition and speak up. Rigor often comes into play here as we dig deep to find the data to back up our intuition. The outermost circle comes from making a practice of listening to and action on our intuition.

Nixon's three concentric circles of reflecting, strategizing, and doing parallel my own cycle of renewing, pursuing, and doing. I broke it down in *The Productive Bite-Sized Entrepreneur* (now available in *The Ultimate Bite-Sized Entrepreneur Trilogy*):

I call the productivity process "pursuing, doing, and renewing." It is an infinite iterative flow where we research our interests, implement our theories, and assess our growth. It is not unlike Eric Ries' landmark Lean Startup method, in which you ship the 'minimal viable product,' or MVP, to get feedback from others as much as possible. In the case of productivity, we're getting feedback from ourselves.

When you think about it, we all do things this way: we think of something, we do it, and then we see if it worked out. When it comes to AGILITY, though, the difference is seeing the potential in something that isn't tied to previous actions. In *The Creative Leap*, Nixon says perspective is "mining the past in order to get insight into the future [while] forecasting requires the practice of inquiry, improvisation, and intuition; it necessitates an ability to toggle between wonder and rigor."

Perspective – seeing how to make the biggest impact because of your previous results – is offered by another precious resource: TIME. On the other hand, forecasting – taking an educated guess as to what should be next – is offered by AGILITY.

The agile-rich and agile-challenged alike do the same cycle of pursuing, doing, and renewing as everyone else, just at quantum levels. To paraphrase Nixon, AGILITY is the high-speed toggle between wonder and rigor, observing and doing, and even trying and failing.

AGILITY is not being paralyzed of potential failure, as you know you'll get another opportunity to choose tomorrow. AGILITY means the opportunity outweighs our sunk costs.

AGILITY assumes that the higher the inputs, the better strategy. Basecamp co-founder Jason Fried says, "In software, people often turn to Apple for design inspiration. It makes sense - the company is wildly successful, it defines trends, and it pushes envelopes. But copying Apple doesn't make you a trendsetter or a rule breaker. It makes you a follower. When everyone mimics Apple, everything tends to look the same. Apple's clean and simple aesthetic is Apple's - it's not yours."

Apple reflects not only the tech ambitions of the late co-founder Steve Jobs, but his time doing transcendental meditation, his time studying history, and his sixties' counterculture aesthetic. The groundbreaking fonts available on the first Apple computers? According to *Becoming Steve Jobs*, they were inspired by a calligraphy class he took in college. Outside influences gave him success in his main field.

Crosspollination adds fuel to the change you seek. I recently talked with serial entrepreneur David Krock. He is an accomplished drummer. When he considers getting involved with a new company, he looks for the rhythm of the business – just as he would anticipate the perfect high-hat or bass drum drop when onstage. I spent my college years DJing, and that pacing – knowing when to let the beat ride, when to let the anticipation build up, and when to change the direction with an entirely new tune – helps me now as a writer, public speaker, and even a one-on-one business coach. When you guide others on their journey, it is priceless to know when to let someone talk, allow an uncomfortable silence, or to ask a question to guide the conversation elsewhere.

There is no wasted experience. They are all valuable in our toolbox.

A great example is fellow DJ D-Nice. The former rapper came into the spotlight with his riveting music sets. The catch: His curated events were all on Instagram. It was Spring 2020, just as America started sheltering-in-place.

From *The Washington Post*:

Last week, Jones woke up at 4 a.m. and, instead of being crippled by the anxiety of the times, decided to throw a party online for his famous pals. With his laptop, signature wide-brim hat and view of Los Angeles ready to go, Jones played music he loved for an Instagram party of about 200 music-industry heavyweights. The next day, 2,000 people joined. Then 12,000. Then 25,000. By Saturday night, more than 100,000 people — including former first lady Michelle Obama and a host of A-listers — were jamming together in "Club Quarantine," the tongue-in-cheek shorthand for the hours-long broadcasts streamed live from Jones's kitchen on his smartphone.

How could he know a pandemic was coming? He couldn't. How could he know he'd become the premier virtual DJ of this era? He didn't.

And he didn't have to.

"I just wanted to do something good for people, and it turned into something really good. It was so unexpected," Jones said in an interview.

Jones' AGILITY wasn't based in the moment. AGILITY is never instantaneous, though it could feel like it to everyone else or even to yourself. It is always rooted in past decisions. I actually grew up with D-Nice. When I was in middle school, his first rap album, *Call Me D-Nice*, was a perennial favorite. As hip-hop eras shifted, Jones became an old-school set live DJ and, later, a professional photographer and music documentarian. Moving the crowd, reading the cultural pulse, and capturing the moment are skills Jones built over time. And when the "Club Quarantine" opportunity presented itself, he was ready.

For the agile-rich and agile-challenged, the boundaries can become blurred between curious exploration and avoidance of rigor. Two tough factors come into play:
- Adding more because we can, and
- Believing something needs to be changed when it just needs to be persevered

Adding more feeds the ego. Sometimes we can identify with the AGILITY and not the practicality of it. Does joining a new club when your dance card is full, being a shoulder to cry on when you don't have the bandwidth, or pursuing yet another creative opportunity when abandoned ones lie in your wake, actually help you nourish the world? Hell, are you even nourishing yourself?

Yes, you may proudly attribute serving others with your busy, hustle nature. Your busyness may also unravel any goodwill you've gained from those you serve. AGILITY can diffuse the impact of what you do.

In *Essentialism: The Disciplined Pursuit of Less*, Greg McKeown says "Essentialists see trade-offs as an inherent part of life, not as an inherently negative part of life. Instead of asking, 'What do I have to give up!?' they ask, 'What do I want to go big on?' The cumulative impact of this small change in thinking can be profound."

Public speaking coach Grant Baldwin puts it like this: "The longer it takes to describe you, the more your speaking fee drops."

He's not just talking about money – he's talking credibility, he's talking potential impact, and he's talking your value to the world. The same is true for investors in your new idea, publishers considering your new book, customers thinking about switching to your new brand, or the community who you are building trust to serve.

The commonality is telling a new person why they should spend time with your vision. It is about getting people as comfortable with your big idea as quickly as possible. And that, of course, reflects the clarity you have with your own vision.

I call it the cocktail test: how would you describe your important vision to someone you just met at a party? I took this quite literally early in my career, and I'd find myself stumbling and fumbling over what, exactly, I was doing as a writer. Every year, though, the vision would get tighter, and before I knew it I could tell people about my intention in one breath. The process began again after I became an entrepreneur, and, after several years, my vision is clear: I'm debunking the myth that you have to sacrifice everything to make your entrepreneurial and creative mark.

Your product isn't for everyone.

Your services can't lift everyone.

And your voice doesn't resonate with all.

Not everyone in your life likes you. Why would what you have to offer be for everyone, either?

True AGILITY begins with purpose. Business coach Marie Forleo's multi-million-dollar empire is built on the first page of *Everything is Figureoutable*: "The power isn't out there, it's in you." Marketer and teacher Seth Godin simply says, "For more than thirty years, I've been trying to turn on lights, inspire people and teach them how to level up." His brilliant Akimbo podcast, online courses, and classic keynote are all built on this simple idea.

Every thing I'm involved in – from keynotes to books to coaching – revolves around my short, focused entrepreneurial creed. This is why you're reading my 25th book. This is how I can make more with less. This is how you can partner with AGILITY. It is simpler for me to adapt, create, and take advantage of new opportunities because I'm providing the same discussion, no matter what the platform. It is also easier for investors, publishers, and communities to understand my vision, bringing better sales and higher investment because they trust my expertise and clarity.

We can also believe something needs to be changed when it just needs to be persevered. Pivoting to a new idea kicks in the adrenaline. It feels good. A pregnant idea is always more romantic than a crying baby. You can't have one without the other, though, and the follow through – what *The Creative Leap* author Natalie Nixon calls transitioning from "wonder to rigor" – is where you bring your worth.

"Your core ideas, those core intentions as a creator, are all built in the struggle, not in the feast," I wrote in *Bring Your Worth: Level Up Your Creative Power, Value & Service to the World*. "The biggest danger, then, isn't missing your oppportunity to shine brightly, to create wealth, or to impact the world, but not allowing the life experiences to prepare you to do those very things. The circumstances will come in disguises, cloaked in a frustrating situation, a setback, or an unexpected development. Your life is tailor made to develop the muscles you need to succeed. The universe doesn't want to punish you, which is as preposterous as believing gravity dislikes skydivers or flames hate firefighters. It is just physics, science, and nature. And, the universe knows exactly when to give you what you need, like a flower always blossoming on time."

We have been fooled into believing trying something new is a risk. It's not. Bravery is picking up the messy pieces from a failure, a mistake, a misstep, and continuing on the journey anyway because it fits, to paraphrase poet Mary Oliver, what you plan to do with your one wild and precious life.

As I talk about with FOCUS, giving up can be great. Giving in, though, doesn't ever make sense.

"The image of the tragic artist who lays down his tools rather than fall short of his impeccable ideals holds no romance for me," Elizabeth Gilbert says in *Big Magic*. "I don't see this path as heroic. I think it's far more honorable to stay in the game – even if you're objectively losing the game – than to excuse yourself from participation because of your delicate sensibilities. But in order to stay in the game, you must let go of your fantasy of perfection."

As a coach, I instinctively get chills when I hear someone talk about "starting over," getting a "clean slate," or "erasing the past." That isn't even possible. As the classic saying goes, "No matter where you go, there you are." Eventually, you're going to have to do that work.

There are things happening beyond your scope. It's not from ignorance or naiveté, but simply because you aren't meant to see them. Your name could be spoken in rooms. Your next best step could be materializing as you read this. Your co-conspirator in a game-changing partnership could be lining up to meet you at your level. You just won't know it until you're supposed to.

AGILITY is trusting you'll be ready when they appear.

How to Partner with Time

I'm bad with time management, but great with attention management. If I'm choosing people and projects that matter to me, then it doesn't matter how long they take.

Adam Grant, The Tim Ferriss Show

One day, I was having breakfast with a friend and they asked, "How do you know when to let something happen and when to *make* something happen?" *I knew* I knew, but I never really articulated it before. I sipped my coffee and paused for a minute. Then I could explain: "Personally, I don't focus on making things happen. I put all my focus on paying attention and watching for the right moment to do it. Then it takes care of itself."

I've created every day for decades, and yet people observing may not realize it is a daily operation – not just when I feel like it. I have a hit about every four years: I do a heavily-citied book, then a couple years pass, then I have a best-seller, and more years pass, and then I co-found a popular app, and so on. In-between those times are flops and duds, quiet work and self doubt, honest conversations with self and others. In-between is creating. In-between is time.

Time affords you the opportunity to think, to create, to fail, and to ultimately impact the culture. If Timing is knowing *when*, Time is knowing *it will*. If I embrace this experience bombing at my first book event, if I spend an evening exploring this thing I'm drawn to, if I give, give, give to the people whom I serve, then all those resources will be at my disposal tomorrow.

I have always been aware of my mortality, well before I experienced any life-threatening situations as an adult. When I wrote, I assumed it would be the last thing I would write. (Something I've found shockingly common among passionate creators.) When I talked to someone, I would sometimes think, "What if this was the last time we say goodbye?" Journalist at 14, high school graduate at 17, grad school graduate at 22. Running like a man on fire.

I understand something different now. Partnering with time isn't about the time you have left or even doing things as quickly as possible, but nourishing the world as much as possible with the time you've got. What this is *not* is public work. This is often silent work. This is often internal work. This is steadfastly building a skill, creating a service, or adding more love, trusting that, over time, your cup will runneth over. Now I can work quietly, with peace, as I know time will naturally accrue the power I need to nourish the world.

You actually have all the time you need. You just have to trust time will give you what you need to make the biggest impact.

Gameplan for Your Time

1. Build a routine
2. Create boundaries. Artificial is fine
3. Set a timeline independent of outside judgment

How to Strengthen Your Time

1. Focus on small wins that build on the results you want later
2. Make decisions based on an easier tomorrow, not an easier right now
3. Remember no matter how hard it is today, it will only be harder to start tomorrow

Boundaries for Your Time

1. Time is not something to fill, but something to leverage
2. Set a personal timeline independent of the time available

Alex Haley knew he had gone too far. Way too far. The late author stumbled upon his family heritage, tracing it all the way back to The Gambia in West Africa. He grew up sitting on a porch in Henning, Tennessee, hearing his Grandma, his Aunties, and other older relatives tell tales of royalty, slavery, and his ancestor, Kunta Kinte.

Fortunately, he listened.

Haley flew to The Gambia with some money he scrapped together and confirmed they were telling the truth: his family roots began there. He got a nice book deal through his literary connections and began writing. And writing. And writing.

He kept writing and traveling and researching until he was tired and broke. In his words, he'd max out all his credit cards and run out of friends to borrow money from, then he'd find a way to make more money and start the process over again.

He also ran faster than the deadline. By his count, he missed the publisher deadline six times. (Doubleday & Company's Editor in Chief Samuel S. Vaughan, in fact, said Haley missed the deadline *nine* times.) Unfortunately, he was no closer to completing his epic family saga. The last time he flew to New York for a deadline extension (and some more advance money), Haley just wrote the most eloquent start to the book, wagering the editor would intensely read the first few pages during his visit to see his progress, and then just trust the rest of the manuscript was coming together. He was right.

Now Haley had just a year – a final year – to complete the massive manuscript pulled together from an estimated 500,000 miles of travel across three continents, hundreds of researched books, and a seemingly infinite number of interviews.

"I could have gone on that way forever, never satisfied that I'd learned quite enough, always hoping that tomorrow I'd stumble across one more piece of evidence that I couldn't do without," Haley told *Playboy Magazine* in 1977, after his book, *Roots*, became the first book in history to sell more than a million hardback copies. "Finally, in exasperation, my attorney, Lou Blau, told me, in so many words, to just stop runnin' my mouth about it, take the research I had – *which was enough for ten books by then* – get off on some desert island somewhere and write the goddamn thing."

And it turned out fine. It usually turns out fine. As long as you actually start.

"It doesn't make any sense to not make something as good as it should be, but we will always be making things that are not as good as they could be, because if we have unlimited time and unlimited money, of course we would make something differently, but we don't have unlimited time and we don't have unlimited money and we must interact with the market," Seth Godin says.

For Haley and other journalists, TIME is our savior and our crucible. We love writing, and, if we find a story we love, we would write forever if we could, peeling away the layers of the onion and getting deeper into the real story. We need a barrier, though. For many of us, our first experience with limitations is the deadline. When does the story need to go to press? When do the editors need it by? When do I have to stop? And our approach becomes based on that limitation, that border, that proverbial stop sign.

But what happens, after years of TIME-based thinking, we are given an assignment that has no deadline? The story sits there. It becomes the neverending story. It will always be published tomorrow. I've been in many newsrooms, and each and every one of us have had at least one story that is important, that is close to our heart, that will absolutely get our full attention once we get the more pressing, deadline-driven articles out of the way.

It is the same for the retiree who no longer has the friction of work to keep him steady, or the long-married divorcee who can't make a decision because she doesn't have someone arguing against her, or the new college student who feels overwhelmed because their parents' rules suddenly don't apply.

We need the friction, the pressure, to perform. It is essential to create deadlines, even if they are artificial.

Before having children, I wrote a dozen and a half books over the course of a decade. After having kids, I wrote seven books in four years, bootstrapped two startups and sold the latter, Cuddlr, within a year an a half, and did my first, as well as my third, TED Talk. It isn't a coincidence. We create within the limits we set. It is just clearer when we have outside influences making this fact tangible.

Off the Clock: Feel Less Busy While Getting More Done author Laura Vanderkam has one of my favorite TIME management stories. A busy mother began tracking her time spent using one of Vanderkam's methods. Suddenly, her water heater broke and flooded her basement. The damage, cleanup, and replacement took several hours out of her week. To her astonishment, though, she still managed to get her weekly activities done – and then some. Somehow she found the time, as if it was lost change under the couch cushion. Necessity breeds efficiency.

TIME is less like a straight line and more like a curve, bending when we're doing something we prioritize. Maximizing TIME is knowing what is important and leaning into those curves. Those curves begin to compress and you progress towards your intention faster.

Vanderkam calls this TIME dividends: you start getting returns based on work you put in before and you are able to get more done faster. We talk about it in her book *Off the Clock*:

"I have been doing my most basic work [writing] for a quarter of a century, so I know exactly how much material and resources I need, just as a veteran craftsman knows the correct amount of wood and nails to build a table." Such knowledge accrues bit by bit. The brain develops muscle memory, which makes much of what would have required deliberation mindless. Brown's insight is this: certain things we do in the present can open up space in the future. These investments of time pay off again and again, much like a stock can pay an annual dividend. People who seem to have lots of time have often structured their lives to create time dividends; as money dividends make a person rich, so time dividends make you feel like this resource is abundant.

What matters isn't how much TIME you have, but what effort you are capable of doing within the TIME you've got. In short, TIME doesn't matter, but the results do. "You can learn a lot from billionaires," basketball-legend-turned-mogul Magic Johnson said in an interview. "The same amount of time it takes to make a million dollars is the same amount of time it takes to make $100 million. Time is key."

The TIME-rich and the TIME-challenged can have the same two blindspots:
- Feeling like TIME is something to fill, rather than something to leverage; and
- Forgetting to set their own timeline independent of the TIME available

The amount of TIME doesn't matter if you aren't building these proverbial muscles. If you want to learn an instrument and don't practice every day, then it doesn't matter if you have a few minutes or several hours available. Building from now means starting where you are with the resources you've got. The Time-rich can believe they will always have tomorrow, while the Time-challenged can believe they will never have enough Time to start.

I learned long ago that it is easier to adjust an oven when you start it already. If I know I'm going to bake, I'll set it to 350 degrees, and then set up my mise en place and pour over the details. Why? Either way, you're going to have to wait for the preheat. You might as well get started. And it's much easier to turn the oven up a few degrees to 375 or down to 325 instead of getting there from a cold oven. And your preheat is the prep, the skills, the Work with a capital "W". "If you want to perform when the world is watching, you have to do the work when no one is watching," Farnam Street's Shane Parrish says. The behind-the-scenes work and details will come together, perhaps quicker than you expect. But you have to put things in motion to have a place to show up once you are ready.

Ironically, not worrying about TIME is the best way to partner with it. Worrying about TIME happens when we use comparative measurements like:
- how long it takes for you to see progress relative to cultural norms,
- how long others believe you should pursue your goal, and
- and how long it should take for you to have outward results.

Saying you have to make some amount of money by, say, age 30 or looking to one-up another peer based on speed are recipes for burnout. What happens if you don't reach these obscure, time-based goals, based on factors not completely in your control? Are you just going to throw it all away? The comparative approach leads us straight into extreme thinking. It's an easy trap to fall into: We have two choices and must absolutely go full throttle into one while leaving the other choice behind. We either stay in a job we hate or quit it to start our own business. We either get married and start a family or dedicate our lives to our careers. There is no flexibility. You're either all in or you give up.

And you must choose now!

Funny measurements pushes us into what psychologist Carol Dweck calls a fixed mindset ("I'm a winner or a loser," all or nothing, pass or fail) rather than a growth mindset ("I will learn from this experience," levels of success, seeing opportunities rather than competitions).

You need to create your own metrics.

When I work with people, the number one reason they are ready to quit isn't because their goal is unrealistic or that they are not ready to do what it takes to achieve it. It is because they haven't accomplished their goal, or made as much progress to their goal, as quickly as they expected. This expectation of TIME is often unconscious.

Motivational speaker Les Brown says you have to water the bamboo tree for years with no sign of life – until, overnight, it suddenly sprouts thick and tall. All the growth is happening underground.

Like your resources, your timeline should be completely based on your personal and professional situation. A side hustler with a 9-to-5 and kids isn't going to create as quickly as an unemployed high school student or a retired grandmother. When I launched my first startup, I knew that my single, tech-inclined friends could do my app in a five-week sprint. My sharpest Silicon Valley friends could have done it in five days. It took me five months.

When you are TIME-challenged, then you need to stretch the timeline to give yourself a proper runway to create. When you are TIME-rich, then you need to shrink the timeline to give yourself a sense of urgency. Both need to create, recognize, and respect limitations.

And Winter 2020 made this abstract distinction very real for Americans. When the Coronavirus pandemic hit U.S. shores, there were immediately two outspoken camps in the creative world. On one hand, the capitalist hamster wheel was finally pausing. Rest as much as possible. No, you don't have to be productive. You can take a well-deserved break. It's a damn pandemic, for God's sake. You better stop while they let you! Otherwise, this was a waste.

On the other hand, the entire world was finally pausing. Get shit done! Yes, you have to be productive. I know you're not going to come out of these weeks, if not months without a new exercise routine (and summer body to go with it), a completed book manuscript, and at least one additional passive income stream. It's a damn pandemic, for God's sake. You better make the most of it! Otherwise, this was a waste.

You either rest like hell or be productive as hell. Any moderation is served with a side of guilt.

Journalist Nora Salem noted a particularly acidic social media message.

On April 2, 2020, Jeremy Haynes, owner of a marketing agency, tweeted:

"If you don't come out of this quarantine with either: 1.) a new skill 2.) starting what you've been putting off like a new business 3.) more knowledge

You didn't ever lack the time, you lacked the discipline"

She says backlash was immediate. "It could have been the timing: With most of the country less than a month into lockdown, and many unemployed or sick or both, Americans were not in the mood to be told that they weren't hustling hard enough…

Everyone, it seemed, agreed that simply surviving the terrifying uncertainty of the moment with physical and mental health intact would be accomplished enough."

But it also speaks to a deeper issue of privilege. We aren't all running the same race. She adds, "[They] often see those who don't have the resources to ensure their health and well-being as lacking the motivation to improve their circumstances, as opposed to facing high structural barrier like lack of inherited wealth, food deserts, or environmental racism."

The truth is that there is nothing extraordinary about this creative time. There was an American pandemic, influenza, exactly a century ago, and at least a half dozen very recent pandemics, from Zika to SARS, that just didn't hit America as hard. The TIME you're spending giving yourself the rest you need, working on your craft, spending with your family, or rebalancing your life was always there. It wasn't given by a pandemic. It was given by you. You gave yourself permission to make the time because you didn't feel judged by others in the world making the same decision to stand within their own priorities.

And this rush to do something isn't because we suddenly have the gift of Time, but from our fear that this Time will go away: You will never get the opportunity again to uproot the political system, nor to create the life you want, nor to bring your neighborhood closer, nor to impact the world. You better act now, because you will never have this much power, opportunity, or influence again.

This simply isn't true.

You don't want to be building a cause in the moment. You want to be continuously creating, brick-by-brick, and have a full-blown blueprint prepared when the world is ready for your message. Those that are telling you to hurry up now are speaking from their own fear – and perhaps tapping into yours.

"We have to understand the interplay between intensity and consistency," says *Start With Why* author Simon Sinek. "You can't go to the gym for nine hours and get into shape. It doesn't work. But if you work out every day for 20 minutes, you will absolutely get into shape. The problem is, I don't know when."

It doesn't mean you don't build now. It means you create for the long game. It means Black Lives will Matter to you in 2030, or sustainable food will still be your intention after the pandemic ends, or the causes you trumpet in your social circles will blanket your timeline as their popularity ebbs and flows.

Yvon Chouinard, founder of the eco-focused clothing company Patagonia, said, "The faster a business grows, the faster it dies. We decided on a growth program so that we would be around 100 years from now. So all decisions were made as if we're going to be around 100 years from now." Frankly, it is far away enough so that you know you'll be dead. Your ENERGY has to lean into creating systems – of beliefs, of actions, of standards – rather than quick fixes.

TIME benefits tremendously from pulling your scope out to the bigger mission. First, it sharpens your intent. Chouinard said, "We slowed down our growth, said 'No' to a lot of opportunities, and became more responsible. In Patagonia's case, it has been a long-time advocate of the environment, supporting global warming prevention initiatives, and donating to aligned causes. Second, daily issues become a lot less petty. Will delaying an action affect your culture 100, ten, or even five years from now? If not, then it's much easier to bypass any hysteria that comes from a minor snafu or setback. Third, it simplifies any overcomplex mission. What basic statement embodies your very purpose? When you think about the next century, what you leave for the world well after you are gone, then the superficial steps, safe platitudes, and popular niceties fall by the wayside.

The spotlight is separate from the creation. Partnering with TIME happens when we remember the difference between the two.

Jay-Z, who began his career a quarter-century ago, explained it to *New York Times*' executive editor Dean Baquet:

The white-hot space is when it is fresh and new, and it's like [clap], "This is the hottest song ever." I stretched that window and I stood in that window for a very long time. [Now], people are not looking to me as 'the thing'... That white hot space, people think it is the biggest thing, but it is really small. It's almost like a trend. Would you rather be a trend or would you rather be forever?

TIME affords you forever.

How to Partner with Energy

Stop measuring your strength by how much shit you can tolerate.

Josie Rosario

My name is Damon Brown, and I am a napper. It started when I finished grad school and became a full-time freelance journalist. It is an independent hustle, pitching publications and offering your services, and you can work from wherever you want. I liked that part. Something romantic about being able to turn in articles from New Orleans one day, then from Tokyo the next day, with my editors being none the wiser. Sure, I was too broke to travel, but I liked to plan. (It would pay off later when I did start world traveling and, much later, became a stay-at-home dad.)

The naps, though. I'm a focused guy, so once I got into the flow, it wouldn't be unusual for me to stay up all night writing or unplug the phone from the wall (as I said, this was a while ago) to go undistracted. I could lean into my biggest resource: FOCUS. Then, I'd go to rest, often with a strong mid-day siesta. On his podcast, Tim Ferriss once talked about a legendary martial arts champ who would take a nap on the sidelines – snoring and all – until right before his fight. Then he'd wake up completely alert and win the match. I felt seen.

But for years, I didn't tell anyone about my daily naps. I wouldn't tell my in-laws, as their tough immigrant culture didn't accept young adults taking siestas. I wouldn't tell my fellow freelancers, as it felt duplicitous to strategize about how to get above the poverty line in one breath and then talk about how refreshed I felt after I spent the afternoon being virtually comatose in the next breath. And I definitely wouldn't tell anyone who didn't believe working from home was an actual job. (This was before WFH, flex days, and the like became fashionable.) So I'd come up with excuses as to why I didn't answer the phone, had to disappear midday, or just wasn't available sometimes.

I knew, though, that napping was an essential part of my energy cycle. My thoughts were clearest mid-afternoon, post-nap, and on well into the night. When I finally moved to New Orleans, I'd wake up mid-morning, nap in the afternoon, and then write my first major book from late afternoon until around midnight. Afterwards, I'd often grab a nightcap with my fellow creative friends in or around the Quarter. I did that for a year. My book manuscript was done shortly after.

I came out about my napping quite a few years back, even calling it essential in my best-selling book, *The Bite-Sized Entrepreneur*. Now colleagues are pleasantly surprised when they listen to their body, actually stop for a moment, and wake up more powerful than before.

Today, entire freaking studies are dedicated to napping. The British Medical Journal, the University of Warwick, and other medical experts found that sleep deprivation – less than six hours a night – can lead to increased heart disease, depression, and other undesired outcomes. A short, hour-or-less nap can help counteract these effects.

I had the wisdom to keep my napping habit for decades. I just wish I was wise enough to listen to myself more and let go of the shame. I'm sure I would have slept a lot sounder.

Gameplan for Your Energy

1. Always have a strategy
2. Choose your battles wisely
3. Use "No." as a complete sentence

How to Strengthen Your Energy

1. Journaling, meditate, or otherwise reflect on your actions
2. Cultivate moments of silence without tech to pay attention to your thoughts
3. Let go of habits that no longer serve you physically, mentally, or emotionally

Boundaries for Your Energy

1. Recognize leaks in your energy
2. Don't mistake stillness for death
3. Know when to let go of an intention

Essentialism author Greg McKeown says the origin of the word "priority" is Greek for "first" or "foremost". There cannot be multiple priorities. There can be primary and secondary, but saying you have a dozen priorities is like saying you are going in a dozen directions. It isn't possible.

It is possible to overanalyze every move you make to the point where you either give up or stop caring out of pure exhaustion. We assume that more choices empower us. In reality, each decision takes more ENERGY away – and can eventually create inertia. It is how you slip into autopilot, perhaps waiting for something big to happen so you can get energized again to take the wheel.

The Paradox of Choice author Barry Schwartz calls this "decision fatigue". In his popular TED Talk, he breaks down three effects of having (or, more accurately, giving ourselves) too many options. First, we tend to procrastinate decisions when the number of choices overwhelms us – and, I would add, the more important the decision, the more likely we are to delay it. Second, we worry about opportunity cost: we're interested in one action, but afraid that we'll miss something else that we can't do as a result. In more modern terms, we'd call this F.O.M.O., or the fear of missing out. Our ever-connected, social-media powered world is ripe with F.O.M.O. opportunities. (ENERGY-conscious folks have come up with one of my personal favorite acronyms, J.O.M.O., or the joy of missing out.) Lastly, Schwartz says we have an escalation of expectations. We made a decision and sacrificed all these other opportunities, so the one we chose *better* be damn good. Schwartz points out that we have more choices than ever, from what ketchup to eat to which type of jeans to buy. That paralysis of analysis has leaked into our personal and professional lives, making us too tired to make the big decisions because we've been, consciously or not, making dozens more little decisions every day.

Like many entrepreneurs and creatives, I hate saying "No". Why? Unlike scientists and other logic-driven people, we don't see the downside. We usually see the possibility.

Unfortunately, saying "Yes" to everything means eventually saying "No" to other things. This is one of the few times when the "scarcity mindset" actually comes in handy: You can't just *make* more TIME, nor can you just make more ENERGY. They will come from something else. You may as well make that a conscious process.

"Opportunities are just obligations wearing an appealing mask," Paul Jarvis says in *Company of One*. "There might be a positive outcome to seizing them, but they always come at a cost – in terms of time, attention, or resources. No matter how hard you try, you can't scale the amount of time in your day. And since you can't somehow buy more hours, you need to find ways to use those hours better."

Saying "No" is the closest thing we've got to creating ENERGY. We know that taking on less with automatically increase our power in what we *do* choose. And yet, we don't say it. In my research, we claim to avoid saying "No" for three reasons:

- We don't want to disappoint others,
- We don't want others to fail without our help, and
- We don't want to miss an opportunity

In reality, it rarely has to do with other people. It has to do with our fear of being free. Without a non-stop agenda, we can feel rudderless and out to sea.

We're in the middle of pandemic time: large swaths of Americans have more TIME than ever before. The same can be said for ENERGY. But we can't escape into social gatherings, we can't hop on a plane to change scenery, and most of us can't dive into our work in the same way. You may have complained about your work commute, doing business trips, or going to a wedding or funeral you would rather avoid. These basic rituals also filled up your day. They created a rhythm. One you don't have anymore.

We're all staring into the void.

"The more accustomed you are to solving problems, to getting things done, to having a routine, the harder it will be on you because none of that is possible right now," University of Minnesota professor emeritus of social sciences Pauline Boss, Ph.D., recently said in an interview. "Our [American] culture is very solution-oriented, which is a good way of thinking for many things. It's partly responsible for getting a man on the moon and a rover on Mars and all the things we've done in this country that are wonderful. But it's a very destructive way of thinking when you're faced with a problem that has no solution, at least for a while."

What is extraordinary about this mass experience is how quickly it exposed our long-standing silent pact: our perceived productivity is directly tied to our self worth. If we aren't busy, then we feel lost.

And if other people aren't happy with their station in life, then they don't have the right to rest.

My 2016 book *The Bite-Sized Entrepreneur* was, in part, a reaction to Silicon Valley productivity shaming. You can do good work, serve your customers, *and* have a life. I saw lots of young men and women buy into the myth that your startup had to be your *entire* life. And then I saw them burn themselves out into oblivion.

Now, we've moved on from judging others on productivity to judging others on how they are productive. Right before the pandemic, there were a slew of thought leaders arguing everyone should wake up at 4 a.m. Apple CEO Tim Cook does it! So does the Seal Team leader who killed Osama Bin Laden! Unsurprisingly, I didn't find one article that gave scientific evidence as to *why*. At least naps have some evidence.

I got up at 3:15 a.m. every morning for two years to run my two startups – because I was primary caretaker of my baby. I still wouldn't argue anyone else do the same.

Seth Godin says culture simply means, "This is how we do things here... [and] what changes culture is each of us: what we expect and how we expect things to go." It doesn't have to make sense. It is just what we decide to believe. That means we can change our minds, too, beginning on an individual level.

"There are so many things that capitalism has stolen, and [one of them is] our dreamspace which is where our power lies," says The Nap Ministry founder Tricia Hersey. "You don't have to work like a dog to get to the end result. You should work towards your calling, but you can work within alignment. You can be balanced. When you're resting and sleeping, you get some of your best ideas for the next move you have to make."

ENERGY-full and ENERGY-challenged people alike can have the same three difficulties:

- Mistaking stillness for death,
- Recognizing leaks in their ENERGY, and
- Knowing when to let go of an intention

Pivot author Jenny Blake talks about being in a "goo" state: The liminal, unclear moment between finishing one action and taking another one. In my *Bite-Sized Entrepreneur* framework, it is the "renewing" part of the renewing, pursuing, and doing creative cycle, as discussed in the AGILITY section.

On her podcast, Blake and spiritualist Penny Peirce described the "goo" state:

Penney equates the liminal space to the time when a caterpillar has created and entered the cocoon, but has not transitioned into a butterfly. It is the space in which we are given the chance to rest, reset, and recharge before moving into the next phase. It sounds lovely when put that way, so why do we often want to rush the process?

But to the caterpillar, stillness is *death*. Just as losing our inefficient routines, dissolving the toxic relationships sapping our ENERGY, and unloading our overbooked schedule feels like a loss of our identities.

The "goo" state – the necessary pause – helps us recognize the leaks in our ENERGY. In my coaching, I've found we usually waste our ENERGY putting the abundance we have or the little we've got into areas in which we have no influence.

We waste our ENERGY trying to gain validation of our work. Our work begins with putting your trust into your instinct, "This particular thing needs to be given to the world and I'm in the position to offer it," and then putting your trust into your audience, "And those whom I want to serve will show up." Doubt in what we instinctively know needs to be given to the world stops us from starting. Doubt in the audience actually showing up keeps us from finishing – and we begin to wiggle, evade, or otherwise drop our best intentions. We try to find ways to secure the win and guarantee our work will be accepted. It means wanting that extra degree or certification to have others take us more seriously (when we really want to validate ourselves), waiting for a major music contract before we take song recording seriously (when we could have been building an audience all along), or investing money in fancy business cards and other paraphernalia (when we haven't sold our first item yet).

We're effectively turning an inside job into an outside job. And we're scattering ENERGY all over the place.

"Our commitment to the process is the only alternative to the lottery-mindset of hoping for the good luck of getting picked by the universe," Seth Godin says in *The Practice*. "A lifetime of brainwashing has taught us that work is about measurable results, that failure is fatal, and that we should be sure that the recipe is proven before we begin. And so we bury our dreams. We allow others to live in our head, reminding us that we are imposters with no hope of making an original contribution."

This is a danger even when we have monumental success. It may even be worse when we have a significant social impact, as it is harder to tune out the outside voices from our inside instinct.

For instance, pop icon Michael Jackson became obsessed with topping his legendary 1983 album *Thriller*. Keep in mind *Thriller* was and is one of the top 20 selling albums *of all time*. As I share in *The Ultimate Bite-Sized Entrepreneur*, his long-time producer Quincy Jones saw him trying to top his record sales – something that was ultimately out of Jackson's control.

The problem? Jackson wanted to do it again. According to Jones, he spent the rest of his life, album after album, trying to create something bigger than Thriller. As a result, he never felt quite satisfied. It is an amazing trap: You naturally hit a home run and, next time up to bat, you're checking wind conditions, wearing a lucky hat and trying to recreate the previous experience. The rub is that what you did - the success you had - wasn't just based on your actions. It is both timing and inspiration, too. The sales success of Thriller *could not be recreated because the whole record industry sold less records, as we would see with Napster and iTunes and Spotify. The needs of the listeners changed (ironically, because of* Thriller *itself), so doing another* Thriller *wouldn't recreate the same sea change. And Jackson was arguably in a different place, as he now had ridiculously high expectations of himself and a new set of pressures.*

There is something unusual about the air on the mountaintop. I've felt lost twice in my life: The year escaping Hurricane Katrina and the year after selling my second startup, Cuddlr. In both cases, my identity – as a Crescent City resident or as a co-founder – and a home – New Orleans or with the Cuddlr community we cultivated – was suddenly gone. It didn't matter if one was by force and the other was by choice. And while I recognize now that the months following Katrina held me in a low-grade PTSD, our sale of Cuddlr showed me how much I identified with the 3:15 a.m. business meetings, constant limelight from the New York Times, WSJ, and other outlets, and the potential of more growth, more community, more opportunities. Suddenly, the light switch turned off. I was no longer a founder. I was just a writer. And perhaps I'd never create again.

So I began to brainstorm new ideas – things I could spin up quickly. I still have a physical journal full of them and a bunch of iPhone notes to match. I'd come up with an idea that I knew would be the next big hit, share it with my confidants, buy the domain name, and so on. Then I'd lose interest. I'd do everything but complete the mockup version so I could actually see if it was worth going deeper on. And then I'd do it again. And again. This went on for weeks.

One day, a friend visited me and we caught up over a long coffee. I breathlessly talked about the Cuddlr experience, the acquisition, and lots of inside baseball that would eventually be shared in some way. Enough of that, I seemed to say, as I have this new idea that will make an even bigger impact. I'm ready to get back in the game.

It was late Fall, and Cuddlr had just sold the previous Summer. I spent almost two years waking up at 3:15 a.m. every morning to found and lead my two companies, So Quotable and Cuddlr, while being a stay-at-home dad and active journalist. I was still primary caretaker of my first son, Alec, now also two years old. And I just found out that we had another son on the way.

"How about this," my friend said, pausing me after I shared my new idea. "What if your family is your startup right now?" It stopped me in my tracks. My family is and was my priority throughout, but I also needed something more. But what if this was my season to be still? Isn't that how So Quotable came about or, when I connected with the two co-founders, how I saw the potential in Cuddlr? It was ENERGY waiting for the best opportunity, not ENERGY scattered trying to make an opportunity. It was trust.

Come to find out, *Inc. Magazine* was looking for a columnist. It became a cathartic way to process my experience and pass along any lessons learned in the whirlwind journey. The column eventually became my self-published best-seller *The Bite-Sized Entrepreneur*. I was now a touring public speaker. And everything happened that brought me here to you right now. But first, I had to let go of my win – the past – and sit still enough to reassess where I should put my ENERGY – my future. I had to stop chasing success.

After her book sold an unexpected 10 million copies, *Eat, Pray, Love* author Elizabeth Gilbert found herself famous, financially secure, and, in her words, stuck. She explained it beautifully in her 2014 TED Talk:

For most of your life, you live out your existence here in the middle of the chain of human experience where everything is normal and reassuring and regular, but failure catapults you abruptly way out over here into the blinding darkness of disappointment. Success catapults you just as abruptly but just as far way out over here into the equally blinding glare of fame and recognition and praise. And one of these fates is objectively seen by the world as bad, and the other one is objectively seen by the world as good, but your subconscious is completely incapable of discerning the difference between bad and good. The only thing that it is capable of feeling is the absolute value of this emotional equation, the exact distance that you have been flung from yourself. And there's a real equal danger in both cases of getting lost out there in the hinterlands of the psyche.

But in both cases, it turns out that there is also the same remedy for self-restoration, and that is that you have got to find your way back home again as swiftly and smoothly as you can, and if you're wondering what your home is, here's a hint: Your home is whatever in this world you love more than you love yourself. So that might be creativity, it might be family, it might be invention, adventure, faith, service, it might be raising corgis – I don't know! Your home is that thing to which you can dedicate your energies with such singular devotion that the ultimate results become inconsequential.

Being famous or prolific won't help you succeed again. What matters is the work and your intention. Is your product or service being done with the audience at the forefront? Are you contributing something more to the cultural conversation? Ego-driven enterprises rarely rise as high as purely-motivated work – and we are in the most danger of doing the former after a big win.

"At some point, the professional has to bring home the fish. That's the fuel that permits the professional to show up each day. But the catch is the side effect of the practice itself. Get the practice right, and your commitment will open the door for the market to engage with your work," Seth Godin says in *The Practice*. "You might seek a shortcut, a hustle, a way to somehow cajole that fish onto the hook. But if it distracts you from the process, your art will suffer. Better to set aside judging yourself until after you've committed to the practice and done the work."

We also waste our ENERGY trying to change someone's mind; it is more effective to change by example rather than argument. In coaching, they say that you can't want your client's success more than they do. A hallmark of my boutique coaching business is that I'm super selective of the people with which I work. I learned early on the cost of taking on a client because they had the money, but didn't currently have the mindset to improve themselves. In one instance, a referral said they wanted to leave their corporate position and launch their own startup. Great, I thought. But then they explained that they were determined to quit their day job as soon as possible, had no entrepreneurship experience, and had no interest in taking on a co-founder because – after I asked a few questions – admitted they wanted as much control as possible.

Let's briefly break down all the alarms that went off: You don't quit your day job based on the promise of potential income. Potential doesn't pay the rent. You cannot understand being a founder until you become one. That's like imagining being a parent when you don't have any kids or thinking what it's like to visit Japan if you've never set foot in Asia. And we co-found companies because it is often too intense to go about it alone and, as was this potential client's case, you need other people to balance your own skills or compensate for all you don't know. In the case of my most notable startup, Cuddlr, it had three co-founders: Charlie Williams as the programming veteran and initial founder; Jeff Kulak as the veteran artist; and me as the media and tech culture veteran. I was the sole founder of my first startup, So Quotable, but I am far from an expert programmer and couldn't draw my way out of a shootout. Our app launched to a 100,000 users in the first week, a quarter million at our peak, and was acquired in a cash deal less than a year after we started. A balanced team doesn't guarantee success, but not having one will almost always guarantees failure.

As gently as possible, I explained all the above to the potential client. They directly rejected each and every insight. This was different, they said. They had an extraordinary idea and the market would carry them where they needed to go, they said. Can I help them? "Not at this point," I say. "But good luck on your journey." (At the time, my bank account wanted to give a different answer.) And then I let them go.

Sometimes you need to let go when other people won't let go. Sometimes you have to protect your own ENERGY leaks when other people won't protect their own.

Several months later, they emailed me out of the blue. They left their job, they built their startup, and, to paraphrase the movie *Field of Dreams*, the people didn't come. Could I help? I could not. As the Greek Stoic Epictetus said, "For it is impossible for a man to begin to learn what he has a conceit that he already knows." This isn't a slam on the potential client, and I did and do wish them the best. I also know that working with them would be a waste of my ENERGY. They are not in a place to receive what I am serving. We all do better when we give sunshine to the plants that are open.

We waste ENERGY building things that aren't built to last; something isn't worth the effort if we have to prop it up 24/7. It reminds me of the old-school Hollywood sets of New York, San Francisco, or a random Western ghost town. You may be able to fool some folks into thinking they've been magically transported to Manhattan, but people are always smarter than we think. And it isn't a passive act: we have to maintain that façade. Think about the one-hit wonder who engineers their entire career to have a big single, a best-selling book, or remarkable fame. The problem, of course, is that these rewards are not permanent, but fleeting. There will always be next week's Billboard chart, tomorrow's New York Times best-seller list, or the up-and-coming starlet taking your place.

"Your audience doesn't want your authentic voice," Seth Godin says. "*They want your consistent voice.*" Your job is to keep showing up, and that's a lot easier if you are true to your own message from the start.

Being who we are is the ultimate ENERGY source. When people ask me how creators like myself can be so prolific, I say it is easier when it comes from the same center. And that center is me being myself. There is no façade. And when people like my work – as a coach, as a keynoter, as an author – then they recognize and trust the consistency across the board and support my work financially across all the platforms. It also means it requires less effort to deliver consistently.

"People can copy skills, expertise, and knowledge, which are all replicable with enough time and effort," Paul Jarvis says in *Company of One*. "What's not replicable is who you truly are – your style, your personality, your sense of activism, and your unique way of finding creative solutions to complicated problems. So lean on that in your work. Sell your *way of thinking* as much as you would a commodity. Polarization can shorten a sales cycle because it forces customers into a quicker binary choice, to decided yes or no. After all, it's hard to make money from maybes."

The ENERGY leaks to get outside validation for our work, to change someone's mind, or to build just for the moment all come from the same place.

Our urges stem from anxiety.

I don't mean the clinical variety. People I care about have generalized anxiety. It is not a condition to be taken lightly. But what I'm talking about is an anxiety of self. We're not sure if we're showing up *right*. And right often means meeting doing what we do with the guarantee that we will be successful. But, of course, there is no guarantee. We persist in looking for it anyway.

"To stay in the present moment takes concentration. Worries and anxiety about the future are always there, ready to take us away," Thich Nhat Hanh says. "We can see them, acknowledge them, and use our concentration to return to the present moment. When we have concentration, we have a lot of energy. We won't get carried away by visions of past suffering or fears about the future. We dwell stably in the present moment so we can get in touch with the wonders of life, and generate joy and happiness."

According to the National Bureau of Economic Research, the pandemic has cut the length of business meetings 20 percent. In other words, a two-hour in-person meeting is now just over an hour-and-a-half. A full-day meeting can adjourn by mid-afternoon. We've already adjusted to remote calls after several months of off-site, virtual meetings, so it's not a matter of so-called Zoom fatigue. What happened?

"The lockdown introduced a host of new problems requiring unplanned, emergent coordination, much of which could be addressed through impromptu interaction if everyone were in the same office," the report says. "With everyone working at home, however, short meetings could serve to quickly communicate new plans, share work that has been accomplished, increase accountability, calibrate priorities, provide social support, and achieve other purposes that are often handled informally in office settings."

"The unplanned, emergent coordination" is why we go to conferences, meet colleagues at coffee houses, and have happy hours with friends. It is the spontaneous exchange of ENERGY and ideas. The ENERGY-full and the ENERGY-challenged also need to remember that these impromptu opportunities can sap away power from any bigger priority. The ENERGY-full can pile on these random interactions, assuming there will be more strength left over to tackle the most important goals, while the ENERGY-challenged may believe that a quick, unexpected detour will take less strength than it actually will.

Now, with a majority of us working from home, we have to boot up our computer or pick up our phone, schedule these interactions onto a calendar or video conference app, and know that every moment we spend within a meeting could be spent doing the actual thing we care most about. As a long-time WFHer, I always knew to prioritize my physical health and rest, my home environment and, later, my family, as they were constantly right in front of me. Now, once-office-bound people realized that they have a choice, too, on where they put their ENERGY.

Lastly, partnering with ENERGY works best when you know when to let go of an intention. Wisdom is knowing when something cost too much compared to what you will get from it.

It reminds me of Seth Godin talking about the difference between price and cost, which I highlight in *The Ultimate Bite-Sized Entrepreneur*: "Price is a simple number. How much money do I need to hand you to get this thing? Cost is what I had to give up to get this. Cost is how much to feed it, take care of it, maintain it and troubleshoot it. Cost is my lack of focus and my cost of storage. Cost is the externalities, the effluent, the side effects."

For the ENERGY-rich, a misplaced or misguided intention is dangerous because you could just keep going and never truly run out of gas. For the ENERGY-challenged, you don't have the ENERGY to waste going in an unintended direction.

And why do we have revelations when we are laying down immobile in a hospital bed, or looking into the tear-filled eyes of a loved one in emotional pain, or unexpectedly getting the pink slip from our job? Because, as Gandalf says in *The Lord of the Rings* movie adaptation, "Thou shall not pass!" It means ENERGY can no longer pass. Sometimes a roadblock is the only way we actually stop to figure out where exactly our ENERGY is going.

The key to both the ENERGY-rich and the ENERGY-challenged is to honor the season you're in: pursuing, doing, or renewing. Renewing means you are reflecting on what you've done and what you'd like to do next. Pursuing means you're strategizing how you'd like to accomplish what you'd like to do next. Doing is the outward manifestation of both.

"I was, and remain, a mighty daydreamer," business consultant and entrepreneur Natalie Nixon says in *The Creative Leap*. "Daydreams are like a magnetic pull for me. What begins as a glance at a small object blurs into the depths of my mind until I pull myself out of my reverie to go back to the matter at hand. I always feel refreshed when I return back to 'normal.' The reverie serves as a type of marinating time for new ideas."

Energy is at its best when it knows where it is going. When put in your best direction, Energy put out multiplies and brings back more than what it left as. It creates what economists call a virtuous cycle. It never ends.

"Understanding your creative power, value, and service is your consistent source, your monk's rope, your allies on this journey. It is the ouroboros, the mythological snake eating its own tail. It is nourished forever," I say in *Bring Your Worth*. "Imagine never retiring, not because you need to work to live, but because you live to work. You live to serve. You feed it, and then it feeds you. Forever. Your job, then, isn't to predict the leap to success, nor to wait for success before you begin. Your job is to serve, and in serving, your true worth will always come to you."

It is the belief that circumstances can and will change, and that your actions, in part, will help make that happen. It is understanding the power of your choices and that you actions aren't going into a vacuum.

Energy is hope.

Buddhist monk Thich Nhat Hanh gives a sublime definition in his book, *No Mud. No Lotus: The Art of Transforming Suffering*:

"When I lived in Vietnam during the war, it was difficult to see our way through that dark and heavy mud. It seemed like the destruction would just go on and on forever. Every day people would ask me if I thought the war would end soon. It was very difficult to answer, because there was no end in sight. But I knew if I said, 'I don't know,' that would only water their seeds of despair. So when people asked me that question, I replied, 'Everything is impermanent, even war. It will end some day.' Knowing that, we could continue to work for peace. And indeed the war did end."

III.
FUTURE'S PAST

HERE, YOU FORGOT SOMETHING

Direction implies exclusion, and exclusion means that very many psychic elements that could play their part in life are denied the right to exist because they are incompatible with the general attitude. The normal man can follow the general trend without injury to himself; but the man who takes to the back streets and alleys because he cannot endure the broad highway will be the first to discover the psychic elements that are waiting to play their part in the life of the collective.

Carl Jung, The Portable Jung

I write this laying on my back in a wobbly tent somewhere in the Nevada mountains. My partner and I are taking our eldest son, who is in the Cub Scouts, and his little brother camping. It is all our first time, sans me going on a quick trip decades ago with my high school best friend and his highly experienced dad. All I can remember is seeing the tent already made, making corny jokes with my friend all night, and waking up to go to Cedar Point.

Now, my middle age (is forty-something middle age? You tell me.) back is sore from laying on the knotted forest floor, aggressively pressing against the tent bottom. My glamping-oriented partner got a queen-sized inflatable bed; but we naively thought our two sleeping acrobats who, seven and four and no more than 50 pounds each, can hardly stay contained with us in our king bed at home, would miraculously fit nicely with sleeping bags. Daddy is laying on the floor. They are all sleep. I am wide awake. A ridiculously howling mountain wind, at least to my New Jersey ears, has been slapping the hell out of our tent. I was first worried about the tent, us flying off like Toto, and, after an hour or so, I realized we weren't going to fly away, especially with the den leaders helping me mallet the hell out of the spikes, and then I worried about my family, as they – well, we – barely slept the night before because our eldest was restless and scared, and I wanted to make sure the noise and flapping and such didn't wake them, but then I realized an hour or so later that I'm closest to the ground and the wall and the violent sounds were biggest to me and me alone.

So instead, I just lay there. I thought about a castle I thought I made up, then I remembered my partner being there and that they were having a party when we passed by, and then I realized it was a memory, but from what country, and then it was a random castle we walked past in Spain many years ago. I smiled.

I thought about loved ones I missed. One in particular spoke to me through the wind, and I suddenly remembered, after his passing, sitting with my sons at our old home, playing in the front yard and feeling his presence, and then I realized how silly it was for me to not connect the heavy storm winds slapping to that very moment long ago. He would have loved this trip. I began to cry.

And then I thought about what took me to this moment to think about moments. The rocky trail up the mountain. The popcorn sales and Pinewood Derby's. Even the seven years of stay-at-home daddying and potty training. All this conspiring for me to be still enough to excavate these memories long forgotten, to bring them to light, to morn them.

And then, I started writing. Some of the passages you've read started pouring out – "downloading", as one of my mentors says. I jammed them into my iPhone, under dim light and heavy wind.

It is now 6:30 a.m. I've been up since midnight.

But these memories and insights came after worrying about the environment (the storm) and the personal (the family). I spent two hours scared about factors outside of my control. I have neither shame nor guilt about it, and I respect it may have been a necessary series of feelings for me to process. I also know it didn't get me any closer to peace. The deep layers hid behind me accepting my boundaries while simultaneously understanding it wasn't forever. It was just now.

It is crucial we pull up what we've forgotten and let go of what is out of our control. The routines, habits, and strengths we carry are not of the future. You learned hyper-FOCUS because you knew what happened when you didn't pay attention - or perhaps from the fear of losing something if you didn't. You built AGILITY because things in your environment made it seemingly impossible to succeed without adapting to new, often unfair parameters. You leveraged TIME because there were others who had the power to take shortcuts, borrow social capital, and create something based on someone else's perceived legacy. You found ENERGY because any action has an equal and opposite reaction, making it paramount to go longer than others who wouldn't have to work so hard to see outward results. These muscles don't just come out of thin air. They come from your experiences. And without honoring all of your experiences, you'll always have an incomplete view of your power – the power you have for yourself and the power you have to unshackle others. In fact, those powers are one in the same.

"I tell my students, 'When you get these jobs that you have been so brilliantly trained for, just remember that your real job is that if you are free, you need to free somebody else,'" said the late Toni Morrison. "If you have some power, then your job is to empower somebody else."

And starts with you letting go of the tools you do not need anymore. Surviving a toxic relationship when you're young, before you had any true agency, can give you awesome resources and seemingly limitless ingenuity. After all, you're trying to survive, so you need to learn how to Focus, be Agile, leverage Time or Energy quickly. But what happens when you or fateful circumstances change the environment? You still carry that power. You also carry the shadow that comes with it. In my favorite passage from *The Power of Onlyness*, Nilofer Merchant says, "To rebel is to push *against*; to lead is to advocate *for*. To rebel is to say 'we won't;' to lead is to say 'we will.' To rebel is to deny the authority of others; to lead is to invoke your own authority. Rebels attack, while leaders drive toward something."

What happens when what you built your whole army to battle is gone?

When what you created a resistance to crumbles?

When what you are resilient against leaves your life?

Everything becomes a war, often without you realizing it, and the toxic cycle continues. Resistance cannot be the foundation of your power. Resilience cannot be the center of your being. Your perceived enemy cannot be a healthy co-conspirator in your identity. And you cannot grow beyond the fight without recognizing the trauma you still carry from it. How can you fully embrace the sun if you aren't recognizing the shadow?

By morning, everyone was fine. Even I was OK despite getting only an hour or two of sleep. When we made it home, I unpacked the car alone and noticed a lump beside our house. It was a pretty, seven-inch bird. It was dead.

I gave it a proper burial.

Take the Build From Now Quiz

Curious about your biggest resource at the moment? Take this quick quiz.

Answer each question as instinctively as possible. Match the answers and see your strongest resource.

For a deeper discovery, go to www.buildfromnowquiz.com.

Then give the book another read and see how you can maximize your strengths in a new light!

1. I worry most about:
    a. Finishing what I start
    b. Missing opportunities because I'm busy
    c. Losing interest in what I begin

d. Obsessing over what I'm into at the moment
2. My friends would say I:
   a. Always follow through
   b. Make the most out of uncomfortable situations
   c. Do things in the most efficient manner
   d. Always go the extra mile when it comes to quality
3. I feel most alive when I:
   a. Work from a blank slate
   b. Push myself harder than I ever have before
   c. Know I have room to learn and correct my mistakes
   d. Deep dive into one concept or idea

If I said:

- 1a & 2a
- 1a & 3d or
- 2a & 3d

Then my biggest resource is Focus

If I said:

- 1b & 2b
- 1b & 3a or
- 2b & 3a

Then my biggest resource is Agility

If I said:

- 1c & 2c
- 1c & 3c or
- 2c & 3c

Then my biggest resource is Time

If I said:

- 1d & 2d
- 1d & 3b or
- 2d & 3b

Then my biggest resource is ENERGY

If I said none of these matches, then my biggest resources are BALANCED at the moment.

Connect with Damon

This book is just the beginning of your growth. Here's how we keep the conversation going.

Get Bonus Content & More

http://www.JoinDamon.me

Get your free business worth toolkit to gain even more insight into your next steps. You'll also get exclusive content, early previews of new goodies, and a weekly discussion with fellow creators!

One-on-One Guidance

http://www.damonbrown.net

I've worked with hundreds of clients and connected with thousands of creatives. I'd love to help you organize your priorities, apply the BUILD FROM NOW method, and make room for your best career. We can set up a time to chat and see if we're a good fit. Reach out at damon@damonbrown.net.

DO THE BITE-SIZED ENTREPRENEUR BOOT CAMP

http://www.bsbootcamp.com

This six-part, self-guided course will bring the best out of your current productivity, focus, and creativity. Taking the book series a step further, THE BITE-SIZED ENTREPRENEUR boot camp is perfect to do at your own pace with my guidance through video, audio, and text. Join through JoinDamon.me to get a special discount on and one-on-one coaching opportunities!

SPEAKING AT YOUR EVENT

http://www.damonbrown.net

I am happy to talk about your event and how a discussion on mindfulness, productivity, or entrepreneurship can best fit your needs. International venues are welcome, as are American events, and my platforms include TED, Colombia 4.0 in Bogota, and American University in Washington D.C. My keynote talks are also available and discussed in detail on the next section, **AVAILABLE KEYNOTE TALKS**.

AVAILABLE KEYNOTE TALKS

Damon is available to speak worldwide at select events, conferences, and companies. His audiences have included the main TED Conference, second stage, in British Columbia, American Underground tech incubator in Durham, NC, Colombia 4.0 in Bogota, Colombia, the Adult Entertainment Expo in Las Vegas, and American University in Washington D.C. Damon's talks interweave personal narrative and industry knowledge with actionable strategies. He is also happy to include Q & As and panel discussion as well as moderating panels and interviewing other leaders.

Watch Damon's speakers reel at www.damonbrown.net.
Contact: damon@damonbrown.net.

PROFIT

HOW TO CREATE YOUR TRUE WORTH

Creatives often undervalue their services to the market, to their bank account, and to the world. In this inspiration and practical talk, Damon shares the best ways we can joyfully make a living off our craft, create business partnerships worthy of our skills, and truly be of service to others.

PRODUCTIVITY

THE POWER OF GOOD ENOUGH

What is the number one killer of innovation? Perfection. With perfection, the key motivation often isn't having high standards, but being afraid of making a mistake. In this talk, I share the three powerful strengths you get when you let perfection go.

Entrepreneurship

Why Your Side Hustle Matters More Than Ever

Believe it or not, we already have most of the skills we need to create our passion-driven business. So why aren't most people pursuing their potentially profitable ideas? They are intimidated by the small gap in their skill set. In this immediately actionable talk, Damon shares how to easily traverse that gap and explains the three crucial strengths every successful entrepreneur possesses. It is an inspiring talk for both potential entrepreneurs and ambitious upstarts.

SIGNIFICANT REFERENCES

I.

AN OUTSIDE JOB

THE LOW END OF THE SOUP BOWL

- Toni Morrison quote: Toni Morrison speech, Portland State University. Spoken May 30, 1975. Transcription published in *Array*, "Toni Morrison on Black Artists". July 9, 2014. Currently available online: http://www.arraynow.com/our-blog-archive/2015/8/13/toni-morrison-on-black-artists
- Violet Blue. *ZDNet*, "Silicon Valley's Race Problem." Originally published October 30, 2011. Currently available online: https://www.zdnet.com/article/silicon-valleys-race-problem/

- *Chani Nicholas,* "Horoscopes for the New Moon in Scorpio – November 2020." Currently available online: https://chaninicholas.com/horoscopes-for-the-new-moon-in-scorpio-2020/

Salmon

- Esther Perel quote: *Steal the Show with Michael Port* podcast, "Unlock Erotic Intelligence in the Bedroom and the Boardroom with Esther Perel." Originally aired December 9, 2015: https://stealtheshow.com/podcast/unlock-erotic-intelligence-esther-perel/
- Chris Rock: *The Daily Show with Trevor Noah.* October 21, 2020. Currently available online: http://www.cc.com/episodes/mdr7q1/the-daily-show-with-trevor-noah-october-21--2020---chris-rock-season-26-ep-26013

- Damon Brown. *Bring Your Worth: Level Up Your Creative Power, Value & Service to the World* (Bring Your Worth 2019).
- Glamour. *Glamour,* "Ava DuVernay's Speech at *Glamour*'s 2019 Women of the Year Awards Must Be Read." Originally published November 12, 2019. Currently available online: https://www.glamour.com/story/ava-duvernay-glamour-women-of-the-year-2019-speech
- Barack Obama: *The Shop: Uninterrupted | President Obama Special.* October 31, 2020. Currently available online: https://www.youtube.com/watch?v=jvy9OWNGPgk
- Thich Nhat Hanh. *No Mud, No Lotus: The Art of Transforming Suffering* (Parallax Press 2014).
- Seth Godin. *The Practice: Shipping Creative Work* (Portfolio 2020).

- Revolt TV, "The Cost of High Fashion" panel with Dapper Dan, Laquan Smith & Jason Bolden. Originally aired November 5th. Currently available online: https://www.youtube.com/watch?v=ZL2tywtSCQg

YOUR SYSTEM IS THE LOCK AND THE KEY

- John Henry quote: *Earn Your Leisure* podcast, "Hustle & Motivate featuring John Henry." Originally aired October 29, 2019: https://youtu.be/o38ZWUK7w9o
- Next Avenue. *Forbes,* "Cindy Gallop: Disrupting Ageism in Advertising." Originally published October 3, 2019. Currently available online: https://www.forbes.com/sites/nextavenue/2019/10/03/cindy-gallop-disrupting-ageism-in-advertising/

- Seth Godin. *The Practice: Shipping Creative Work* (Portfolio 2020).

UNDERSTANDING THE FATES

- Thich Nhat Hanh quote: *No Mud, No Lotus: The Art of Transforming Suffering* (Parallax Press 2014).
- The Systems Thinker. *The Systems Thinker*, "The Ladder of Inference." Volume 10. Currently available online: https://thesystemsthinker.com/the-ladder-of-inference/
- Don Miguel Ruiz: *The Four Agreements: A Practical Guide to Personal Freedom* (Amber-Allen Publishing 2018).
- Damon Brown. Adapted from the *Inc. Magazine* column, "The Strongest Leaders Use This Simple, Powerful Phrase." Originally published May 31, 2016. Currently available online: https://www.inc.com/damon-brown/the-

strongest-leaders-use-this-simple-powerful-phrase-.html
- Damon Brown. *The Ultimate Bite-Sized Entrepreneur Trilogy: 76 Ways to Boost Time, Productivity & Focus On Your Big Idea* (Bring Your Worth 2017).

II.

AN INSIDE JOB

HOW TO PARTNER WITH FOCUS

- Julian Mitchell quote: *#ChopItUpShow.* "The Business Behind Music and Culture with Julian Mitchell," Episode 10. Originally aired November 11, 2018: https://youtu.be/M8gSvpas6GE
- Damon Brown. *The Bite-Sized Entrepreneur Trilogy: 21 Ways to Ignite Your Passion & Pursue Your Side Hustle* (Bring Your Worth 2016).

- Simon Sinek. *The Infinite Game* (Portfolio 2019).
- Damon Brown. Adapted from the *Inc. Magazine* column, "How Perfectionism is Preventing You from Perfection." Originally published February 28, 2018. Currently available online: https://www.inc.com/damon-brown/how-perfectionism-is-preventing-you-from-perfection.html
- Elizabeth Gilbert, "Success, failure, and the drive to keep creating," from TED. (TED Talks, March 2014). Currently available online: https://www.ted.com/talks/elizabeth_gilbert_success_failure_and_the_drive_to_keep_creating/
- Seth Godin. *The Practice: Shipping Creative Work* (Portfolio 2020).
- Damon Brown, "Why you should strive for good enough," from TEDxToledo. (TED Talks, September 2018).

Currently available online: https://www.ted.com/talks/damon_brown_why_you_should_strive_for_good_enough

- Seth Godin. *The Dip: A Little Book That Teaches You When to Quit (and When to Stick)* (Portfolio 2007).
- Stephen Covey. *First Things First* (Mango Media 2015).
- Elizabeth Alexander, "Creative process: Are you in a period of 'woodshedding'?," from Big Think. (Big Think, April 2020). Currently available online: https://bigthink.com/creative-process-2645857657
- Damon Brown. Adapted from the *Inc. Magazine* column, "A Thanksgiving Story That Will Save You Time and Money." Originally published November 21, 2016. Currently available online: https://www.inc.com/damon-brown/a-

thanksgiving-story-that-will-save-you-time-and-money.html
- Jessica Dore. *Jessica Dore*, "October 2020 Tarot Offering." Currently available online: https://www.jessicadore.com/offerings/october-2020-tarot-offering
- Elizabeth Gilbert. *Big Magic: Creative Living Beyond Fear* (Riverhead Books 2015).
- *The Bill Murray Stories: Life Lessons Learned from a Mythical Man* (Double Windsor Films/Old Lime Productions 2018). Directed by Tommy Avallone. Trailer currently available online: https://www.youtube.com/watch?v=XC2WIXtWgoc

How to Partner with Agility

- Chase Jarvis quote: *The Chase Jarvis Show*. "Creative Therapy with Seth Godin in New York," Episode 172 Originally aired October 16, 2019: https://www.chasejarvis.com/project/chase-jarvis-live-podcast/
- Damon Brown. Adapted from "The Lonely Road". Featured in *The CNF Audio Mag: Issue 1* (Brendan O'Meara 2019).
- *Drink Champs*. "Busta Rhymes on Working With Mariah Carey, Janet Jackson, His New Album & More." Originally aired October 31, 2020: https://www.youtube.com/watch?v=i7nieCNVbE4
- Natalie Nixon. *The Creative Leap: Unleash Curiosity, Improvisation, and Intuition at Work* (Berrett-Koehler Publishers 2020).

- Damon Brown. *The Ultimate Bite-Sized Entrepreneur Trilogy: 76 Ways to Boost Time, Productivity & Focus On Your Big Idea* (Bring Your Worth 2017).
- Damon Brown. Adapted from the *Inc. Magazine* column, "Why You Should Have More Than One Career at the Same Time." Originally published February 28, 2018. Currently available online: https://www.inc.com/damon-brown/why-you-should-have-more-than-one-career-at-same-time.html
- Helena Andrews-Dyer. *The Washington Post,* "Celebrity DJs' live online sets have become house parties for the homebound: Welcome to Club Quarantine." Originally published March 24, 2020. Currently available online: https://www.washingtonpost.com/arts-entertainment/2020/03/24/dj-dnice-club-quarantine-parties/
- Greg McKeown. *Essentialism: The*

Disciplined Pursuit of Less (Currency 2014).

- Damon Brown. Adapted from the *Inc. Magazine* column, "How to Sell Better in 13 Simple Words." Originally published March 3, 2020. Currently available online: https://www.inc.com/damon-brown/how-to-sell-better-in-13-simple-words.html

- Marie Forleo. *Everything is Figureoutable* (Portfolio 2019).

- Seth Godin. *Seth's Blog*, "About Seth's Godin." Currently available online: https://seths.blog/about/

- Damon Brown. *Bring Your Worth: Level Up Your Creative Power, Value & Service to the World* (Bring Your Worth 2019).

- Elizabeth Gilbert. *Big Magic: Creative Living Beyond Fear* (Riverhead Books 2015).

How to Partner with Time

- Adam Grant quote: *The Tim Ferriss Show*. "Adam Grant – The Man Who Does Everything (#399)." Originally aired December 5, 2019: https://tim.blog/2019/12/05/adam-grant/
- Murray Fisher. *Playboy*, "The Playboy Interview: Alex Haley by Murray Fisher." Originally published January 1977. Currently available online: https://alexhaley.com/2019/06/06/alex-haley-interviewed-by-playboy/
- Edwin McDowell. *New York Times*, "Publishing: Dealing with the Delinquent Author." Originally published July 22, 1983. Currently available online: https://www.nytimes.com/1983/07/22/books/publishing-dealing-with-the-delinquent-author.html
- Laura Vanderkam. *Off the Clock: Feel*

Less Busy While Getting More Done (Portfolio 2018).

- Shane Parrish. *Farnam Street*, "If you want to perform when the world is watching, you have to do the work when no one is watching." Originally published October 1, 2020. Currently available online:

  https://www.instagram.com/p/CFzilkOprOH/?igshid=wzukrxmnuijq

- Carol Dweck. *Mindset: The New Psychology of Success* (Ballentine Books 2007).

- Les Brown, "How Bamboo Trees Will Bring Out Your Best Self," from Goalcast. (July 2018). Currently available online: https://www.goalcast.com/2018/07/10/les-brown-how-bamboo-trees-will-bring-out-your-best-self/

- Nora Salem. *Bitch Media*, "To Well and Back: The Bleak Future of Positive

Thinking." Originally published October 28, 2020. Currently available online: https://www.bitchmedia.org/article/goodbye-to-the-wellness-grift

- Damon Brown. Adapted from the *Inc. Magazine* column, "This is Simon Sinek's Guaranteed Secret to Success Most of Us Won't Do." Originally published July 30, 2018. Currently available online: https://www.inc.com/damon-brown/this-is-simon-sineks-guaranteed-secret-to-success-most-of-us-wont-do.html
- Damon Brown. Adapted from the *Inc. Magazine* column, "Forget Five Years. Make the 100-Year Plan." Originally published November 10, 2017. Currently available online: https://www.inc.com/damon-brown/the-five-year-plan-is-old-what-are-you-doing-in-a-century.html

- *The New York Times.* "Jay-Z and Dean Baquet, in Conversation." Originally aired November 30, 2017. Currently available online: https://www.youtube.com/watch?v=XbuQAbG2AZ0

HOW TO PARTNER WITH ENERGY

- Josie Rosario quote: "Stop measuring your strength by how much shit you can tolerate." Originally published November 19th. Currently available online: https://www.instagram.com/p/CHxRcX4AsRZ/?igshid=8rtgszo044kl
- Damon Brown. *The Bite-Sized Entrepreneur Trilogy: 21 Ways to Ignite Your Passion & Pursue Your Side Hustle* (Bring Your Worth 2016).
- Greg McKeown. *Essentialism: The Disciplined Pursuit of Less* (Currency

2014).

- Barry Schwartz, "The Paradox of Choice," from TED. (TED Talks, July 2005). Currently available online: https://www.ted.com/talks/barry_schwartz_the_paradox_of_choice/
- Damon Brown. Adapted from the *Inc. Magazine* column, "Why the Most Successful Creatives Love Daily Routines." Originally published December 17, 2019. Currently available online: https://www.inc.com/damon-brown/why-most-successful-creatives-love-daily-routines.html
- Seth Godin. *The Practice: Shipping Creative Work* (Portfolio 2020).
- Paul Jarvis. *Company of One: Why Staying Small is the Next Big Thing for Business* (Mariner Books 2019).
- Tara Haelle. *Elemental*, "Your 'Surge Capacity' Is Depleted – It's Why You Feel Awful." Originally published August 13,

2020. Currently available online: https://elemental.medium.com/your-surge-capacity-is-depleted-it-s-why-you-feel-awful-de285d542f4c

- Tricia Hersey. *The Nap Ministry*, "There are so many things that capitalism has stolen, and [one of them is] our dreamspace which is where our power lies..." Originally published October 12, 2020. Currently available online: https://www.instagram.com/p/CGQoexrl6rk/?igshid=1b8ehOnggxqs7

- *Pivot Podcast with Jenny Blake.* "124: Penny & Jenny Show – Embracing Liminal Space (the In-Between)." Originally aired July 7, 2019: http://www.pivotmethod.com/podcast/liminal-space

- Damon Brown. *The Ultimate Bite-Sized Entrepreneur Trilogy: 76 Ways to Boost Time, Productivity & Focus On Your Big Idea* (Bring Your Worth 2017).

- Elizabeth Gilbert, "Success, failure, and the drive to keep creating," from TED. (TED Talks, March 2014). Currently available online: https://www.ted.com/talks/elizabeth_gilbert_success_failure_and_the_drive_to_keep_creating/
- Thich Nhat Hanh. *No Mud, No Lotus: The Art of Transforming Suffering* (Parallax Press 2014).
- Jessica Stillman. *Inc. Magazine,* "The Pandemic Is Making Meetings Less Awful." Originally published August 12, 2020. Currently available online: https://www.inc.com/jessica-stillman/the-pandemic-is-making-meetings-shorter-workdays-longer-new-study-finds.html
- Natalie Nixon. *The Creative Leap: Unleash Curiosity, Improvisation, and Intuition at Work* (Berrett-Koehler Publishers 2020).

- Damon Brown. *Bring Your Worth: Level Up Your Creative Power, Value & Service to the World* (Bring Your Worth 2019).

III.

A FUTURE'S PAST

HERE, YOU FORGOT SOMETHING

- Carl Jung quote: Carl Jung, edited by Joseph Campbell. *The Portable Jung* (Penguin Classics 1976).
- Pam Houston. *Oprah Magazine*, "The Truest Eye." Originally published November 2003. Currently available online: https://www.oprah.com/omagazine/toni-morrison-talks-love/
- Nilofer Merchant. *The Power of Onlyness: Make Your Wild Ideas Mighty Enough to Dent the World* (Viking 2017).

Acknowledgements

Every creation is a group effort, the collective sum of countless conversations, quiet confirmation, and public will. BUILD FROM NOW is no exception.

Thank you to my long-time friend and editor Jeanette Hurt as well as the great cover designer Bec Loss of The Bec Effect. I've loved collaborating with y'all since I went independent, all the way back to the original *Bite-Sized Entrepreneur*. A big hug to my best friend and amazing musician, Purple Fluorite ne A. Raymond Johnson, and wise media producer Neha Tiwari of Version Consulting for putting together the speaker reel to celebrate the book launch. I'm excited to be part of the journey to you doing bigger and better things.

I appreciate the many conversations with

Nilofer Merchant, Jenny Blake, Will Lucas, Jeanette Brown, Jenny Fink, E.B. Boyd, Sherry Paprocki, and my mentors, coaching clients, and supporters giving feedback on the concept. Because of y'all, the book shines a little brighter.

A hat tip to *Inc. Magazine*'s Laura Lorber and Mark Coatney, *CNF Podcast*'s Brendan O'Meara, *Fatherly*'s Tyghe Trimble, *Paperwork Studios*' Andrew Burmon, *GEN*'s Max Ufberg, *Costco Connection*'s Steve Fisher, *ASJA Magazine*'s Stephanie Vozza, Toledo-Lucas Public Library's Jason Kucsma, Tim Hagen, and Linda Fayerweather, Bedroom Kandi's Rita Silva-Grondin, and Bloom Anywhere's Gwen Moran for the opportunity to publicly explore this big idea.

Appreciation to the many luminaries cited in BUILD FROM NOW, from those I'm fortunate to know, like Julian Mitchell and Laura Vanderkam, to those whom I wish I had a chance to know, like Alex Haley and Toni Morrison. Perhaps one day.

Thanks to Akimbo's The Marketing Seminar workshop which I attended as I wrote BUILD FROM NOW. Seth Godin has always been a mentor from afar, and it was priceless to work more intimately with him and my cohort.

And blessings to Catherine Johnson, Amar Brown, and loved ones who transitioned beyond the here and now. I am glad you are without pain. And I still feel your presence and love every single day.

About the Author

Damon Brown helps side hustlers, solopreneurs, and other non-traditional creatives bloom. As a best-selling author, two-time startup founder, and four-time TED Speaker, Damon co-founded the popular platonic connection app Cuddlr and led it to acquisition within a year, all while being the primary caretaker of his infant son. He now guides others through his one-on-one business coaching, *Inc. Magazine* column <www.incdamonbrown.com>, and side hustle bootcamp <http://paylancing.teachable.com>. Most recently, Damon was the first Entrepreneur-In-Residence at the Toledo Library.

His popular keynotes build a conversation around work-life balance, personal success, and supporting diverse talent. Inc., Salesforce, and Google have hosted his in-person and off-site talks. You can watch his keynotes at www.damonbrown.net.

BUILD FROM NOW is his 25th book.

His notable titles include the *Build From Now* precursor *Bring Your Worth: Level Up Your Creative Power, Value & Service to the World* (Bring Your Worth Publishing 2019), the best-selling *The Ultimate Bite-Sized Entrepreneur Trilogy* (Bring Your Worth Publishing 2017) as well as the coffeetable book *Playboy's Greatest Covers* (Sterling Publishing 2012).

You can catch Damon in *Playboy*, *Fast Company*, and *Costco Connection*, as well as at any locale that serves really spicy food. He lives in Las Vegas, Nevada, with his wife, two young sons, and countless bottles of hot sauce.

Connect with him at www.JoinDamon.me or on Twitter/Instagram at @browndamon.

www.ingramcontent.com/pod-product-compliance
Lightning Source LLC
Chambersburg PA
CBHW072145100526
44589CB00015B/2099